THE DAY
DONNY HERBERT
WOKE UP

THE DAY

DONNY HERBERT

WOKE UP

A True Story

RICH BLAKE

HARMONY BOOKS / NEW YORK

Harmony Books is a registered trademark and the Harmony
Books colophon is a trademark of Random House, Inc.

Library of Congress Cataloging-in-Publication Data
Blake, Rich.
The day Donny Herbert woke up: a true story / Rich Blake.—
1st ed.
1. Herbert, Donny—Health. 2. Coma—Patients—United
States—Biography. 3. Fire fighters—United States—
Biography. I. Title.
RB150.C6B57 2007
362. 196'8490092—dc22   2007015220
[B]

ISBN 978-0-307-38316-7

Printed in the United States of America

DESIGN BY LENNY HENDERSON

10 9 8 7 6 5 4 3 2 1

First Edition

For Donny, Tommy, Patrick, and Nicholas

And in all things whatsoever
you shall ask in prayer,
believing, you shall receive.
—SAINT MATTHEW, 21:22

THE DAY
DONNY HERBERT
WOKE UP

Prologue

THE SMALL PARISH of St. Agatha is located on the north end of Buffalo's predominantly Irish Catholic south side. It's a scrappy neighborhood, a dozen or so residential streets interlocking in the shadow of an abandoned steel plant and a tremendous swath of railroad yards. St. Agatha's is less than one mile from the grassy marshlands of the Tifft Nature Preserve, an incongruous but welcome buffer from pungent industrial sites along the eastern shore of Lake Erie. Here, small marinas share the waterfront with rusted-out grain elevators, towering totems of the city's long-ago flour-milling heyday.

St. Agatha's Church is a simple, beige-brick rectangular structure better suited for a post office than a house of worship, but despite spartan, basement-level confines, it's comfortable. Many of the surrounding two-family homes are weathered brick and wood-frame structures, narrow, set close together, a reason this neighborhood historically has always remained so tight-knit. In recent years, as older residents left or died, the area gradually deteriorated and the number of weekly churchgoers dwindled. The youth of the neighborhood, who run the full gamut from Little Leaguers in brush cuts to obese punkers in black, stalk the fading commercial stretches of South Park Avenue and Abbott Road, where corner taverns and pizzerias stubbornly offset vacant lots and boarded-up storefronts.

On Friday nights, some parishioners make their way to the Buffalo Irish Center, just a few blocks away from the church. Built in the 1920s as a YMCA, it was converted in the early 1970s into a pub and gathering hall for the South Buffalo Irish—the Gaelic American Athletic Association, labor figures, politicos, the organizers of the annual St. Patrick's Day Parade. On most nights there's an overflow of draft Guinness in thick pint glasses to be consumed along with lively folk music performed by the likes of Penny Whiskey and the Blarney Bunch.

On this particular evening, Friday, April 29, 2005, the Irish Center is host to a special gathering. Among those seated around folding tables in the plain but spacious backroom banquet hall is the party's host, Linda Herbert, who is accompanied by her three young sons, Thomas, twenty-two, Patrick, twenty, and Nicholas, thirteen. Both her husband, Donald, and her eldest son, Donald Jr., are absent. The latter Herbert, a restless twenty-three-year-old, is on a backpack adventure halfway around the world.

His father is in another world altogether.

Linda is surrounded by a hundred or so smiling relatives, neighbors, and old family friends. She's thrown this party for her parents, Jack and Mary, who are marking their fiftieth wedding anniversary. Linda has planned this party for weeks, and all of her ten siblings—and their children, too many to count—have come to join them in the celebration. A video montage plays on a big-screen television, casting a warm spell. Vintage photographs movingly chronicle the close family's lifetime of simple joys—Christmas mornings, camping trips, graduation parties. Set to Kenny Rogers's "Through the Years," the video generates its own soundtrack of laughter and exclamations around the room, each photo igniting fond memories.

Then it appears. To an outsider it might seem like just another old snapshot. But not to those in the room.

It is the faded image of Linda and her husband, Donny, laughing and dancing together on the occasion of Jack and Mary's fortieth anniversary party in 1995. A silent sadness fills the room.

Over roughly the past decade since that photograph was taken, Donny Herbert has been in a nursing home, confined to a wheelchair in an unresponsive stupor. He is, in the cruelest of terms, a *vegetable*.

Donny is oblivious to the world around him. He doesn't speak. It is believed that he cannot see, although his eyes are open in waking hours. One side of his gaunt face is frozen in a grimace, his right eye flinching upward as if struggling to look away from something sinister. Donny

Herbert is so drastically unlike the energetic, ruggedly handsome firefighter he once was that some find it a struggle to look at him.

Donny has been this way since late December of 1995, when the roof of a burning building caved in and trapped him without oxygen for six minutes. His fellow firefighters pulled him, unconscious, from the charred debris. Barely alive, hooked up to life support, he would eventually emerge from a coma; Donny, however, was gone.

As this photo, this wrenching reminder of better days, disappears, Linda fights back her tears, keeping it together as she always has for her children. She is not alone in her anguish. In that uncomfortably quiet moment, most everyone in the room thinks about Donny.

How tragic.

Why Donny?

Those poor kids.

Some in the room that night, including Linda's mother, Mary, her sister Teresa, and her aunt Ellen, would later describe how right at that heartbreaking moment, they each had prayed quietly for Donny, as they had done so many times throughout these difficult years. Those who loved Donny, and there were many, had never stopped praying for him.

For a miracle.

One

O N   A   C H I L L Y   F R I D A Y   afternoon just before Christ-mas 1986, Donny Herbert kissed his young wife, Linda, on the forehead, bear hugged his three toddler sons, and set off for his first-ever shift as a Buffalo firefighter. For the twenty-five-year-old Seneca Street kid, this was one of the proudest days of his life. Donny might not have gone to college, but he *was* the first member of his family to join the department. The written and physical tests, months of limbo waiting for a slot, eight difficult weeks at the Buffalo Fire Department Training Academy—all of it had led to this moment. Donny intentionally took his time putting on his official uniform—navy blue button-down shirt, navy blue pants, black dress shoes. He packed his '84 Chevette hatchback with his personal set of BFD turnout gear and waved good-bye.

"Good luck," Linda called from the front-porch door-way of their rickety Spaulding Street duplex, the shouting of the children drowning her out. Don Jr., a happy-go-lucky St. Agatha's kindergartner, was particularly amped up.

"Daddy's gonna ride on the fire trucks!" he yelled as his younger brothers, Tommy and Patrick, parroted him, the three youngsters popping up and down like a set of firing pistons.

In a few days Donny would start an official four-day tour as a member of the department's second platoon, which meant a rotating schedule consisting of two nine-hour day shifts (eight A.M. to five P.M.) and two fifteen-hour evening shifts (five P.M. to eight A.M.), followed by four days off in a row. He was being thrown into the mix mid-cycle, starting with an overnight stint. Donny was assigned to Ladder 6, housed along with Engine 21 on the corner of Best Street and Earl Place in one of the worst of Buffalo's East Side neighborhoods. No matter; Donny looked forward to life at that firehouse, a two-story hilltop outpost of red brick. "The Hill," as it was known in the department, was more than a century old and located one block east of War Memorial Stadium, an unused concrete monolith nicknamed "the Rockpile." Donny embraced his new career with his usual enthusiasm, setting out for work more than an hour early. Donny had made roughly the same money, around twenty thousand dollars a year, at his old job, as a machinist at a Ryder manufacturing plant. But cutting steel and fashioning parts was brutally tedious work and not what Donny saw himself doing for the rest of his life.

As Linda turned to go back inside, she, too, was excited for Donny, though she realized suddenly that his being gone all night would take some getting used to. One thing she was not, however, was worried.

About fifteen minutes later, Linda was debating the expediency of fish sticks versus Hamburger Helper when a Channel 7 Eyewitness News bulletin flashed across the bottom of the television screen: St. Mary's Church on Buffalo's East Side was ablaze and had just gone to a third alarm. Outside, Linda could hear sirens. If fire trucks from South Buffalo were heading over, then this could be a five-alarm fire, she thought. Linda had absorbed a fair amount of information about the department during the past two months while Donny was at the academy. Now she was getting her first real lesson in what it was like to be a fireman's wife.

BUILT OF TIMBER AND LIMESTONE by German immigrants and consecrated in 1859, St. Mary's Redemptorist Roman Catholic Church was, in a city noteworthy for its architecture, a remarkably beautiful structure. Though hardly a cavernous cathedral at just 186 feet long and 81 feet wide, the church nevertheless became a striking component of the ever-rising nineteenth-century Buffalo skyline. Indeed, St. Mary's 240-foot steeple tower on the corner of Broadway and Pine Streets was for many years one of the highest points in the city. During the neighborhood's own high point, just after World War II, St. Mary's claimed thousands of parishioners, many of them working-class or poor. They looked to the gray stone edifice of St. Mary's, with its magnificent stained-glass panels and towering copper spire, as a fortress of comfort and refuge. Weekly Wednesday night novenas drew thousands of Catholics from around the city. Devout visitors often described an almost uncanny spiritual warmth emanating from inside. Regardless of whether any of them ever realized it, the church was believed to be sitting on particularly hallowed ground: the exact birthplace of Monsignor Nelson H. Baker, once vicar general of the Catholic Diocese of Buffalo and the region's most revered spiritual figure. By the time of his death in 1936 at age ninety-four, Father Baker had garnered worldwide attention over tales of unexplained "miracles" and mysterious healings. Long after Father Baker's death, dozens of stories of miraculous medical recoveries were linked to his answered prayers.

In the 1950s and 1960s, as families of German and Polish descent migrated in droves farther eastward to the suburbs of Cheektowaga and West Seneca, St. Mary's was reborn as a spiritual hub for black Catholics and the black community overall. But by the 1970s, the church had fallen into disrepair, much like the neighborhood itself, corroded by debilitating poverty, crime, and neglect. In June 1981, Bishop Edward Head decided to officially shut down the church, its regular parishioners by then numbering fewer than a hundred. The building and adjoining property were subsequently sold to a private developer, who announced demolition plans.

An effort was undertaken by concerned community members to stave off the wrecking ball. St. Mary's received one temporary reprieve after another as politicians and volunteers fought to save it, eventually convincing the city to grant the church official landmark status. Meanwhile, the abandoned complex, which consisted of the church, a convent/orphanage, and a rectory, as well as a completely gutted three-story trade school, became a nesting ground for vagrants and winos who circumvented fences and welded-shut doors in increasingly creative fashion. As the weather turned colder, the unauthorized inhabitants set trash-can fires to stay warm at night. By morning the flames would relent, leaving a putrid, smoky stew of ash and blackened garbage. On Friday, December 19, 1986, one such discarded fire refused to merely smolder.

AT APPROXIMATELY 2:45 P.M., a passerby noticed smoke pouring out the back of St. Mary's Church and pulled the alarm box across the street. Right on the fringe of downtown Buffalo in an area teeming with degenerates and hoodlums, the fire alarm box on Broadway and Pine was always going off. The call initially warranted an abbreviated response unit, a couple of four-man engine companies and a ladder truck. A crew from Engine 1 on South Division and Ellicott, a few blocks away, arrived on the scene first. Firefighters realized within minutes that this was no false alarm.

The fire had spread from the empty brick school building behind St. Mary's into the church itself, traveling quickly across superheated air pockets between the ceiling and roof. Soaring dark orange flames ignited the rafters of the church. Once it met that wide-open area, the fire became impossible to contain. A row of decrepit wooden homes sat adjacent to St. Mary's to the rear. With a stiff wind whipping off Lake Erie, not only was a sacred piece of Buffalo's history in grave danger, but a large section of Pine Street was as well.

NOT LONG AFTER Donny Herbert pulled into the parking lot behind the Ladder 6/Engine 21 firehouse, it was apparent that his first day on the job was not going to be spent in the kitchen playing cards and drinking coffee. Both sides of the vintage double house were empty; rigs, equipment, and firefighters were already at the St. Mary's fire. A few of the other guys on second platoon began to trickle into the vacated apparatus floor around 4:15 P.M. It was quiet except for the muffled static of radio traffic. Firefighter Greg Pratchett, a three-year veteran but around the same age as Donny, welcomed the rookie aboard and instructed him to gear up. Someone would be coming in the division chief's rig to take them over to the fire. Pratchett, who moonlit as a substitute teacher, had stopped by St. Mary's on his way to the firehouse. He gave Donny and the other two second platoon guys assigned to Ladder 6, Ricky

Bryant and Dave Perry, a quick rundown of what was going on. "Surround and drown," Pratchett summarized.

By 4:20 P.M., the fire had drawn a dozen engine companies from around the city, as well as four ladder trucks, both rescue units, and all the senior officers, including division and battalion chiefs, the commissioner, and the deputy commissioner. Some men in a fire department will never see a five-alarm fire during their entire career. Donny was about to take part in one on his first day.

The late December sun had not quite set, but the sky was already pitch-dark with smoke. A transfixed crowd of onlookers, including many streets department workers who were just then punching out of a massive garage on the next block, gathered in all directions to watch the show: spectacular, rolling flames utterly devouring the church. At 4:27 P.M. one of four clocks adorning each side of the steeple tower blew out with a loud pop and shot into a nearby yard like a streaking comet. In the fleeting light of early winter, the legions of spectators and firefighters were all looking skyward. The breathtaking spire would most certainly topple.

Fire Commissioner Al Duke got on the radio and ordered the firefighters to pull back to the rear of the church. Engine 18, which was pumping from a hydrant right in front of the church, promptly disconnected and moved farther down Pine Street. Ladder 6, an old-style tiller truck, was also relocated from a precarious position.

As the new guy, Donny was given little to do other than stick close to Pratchett, who served as acting lieutenant in the absence of Captain Don Stoeckel (who was finishing up some paperwork at the training bureau). From the tiller seat, Pratchett operated a powerful ladder pipe hose aimed at the church. Thick, menacing flames, accompanied by hellish black smoke, continued to climb up the sides of the steeple tower and licked toward the very top, a metal sphere sporting a tiny cross.

A few minutes later there came another frightening blast that sent a ball of flames roaring into the dusk, almost as if it had been belched from the side of the tower by some imaginary blowtorch. "It's only a matter of minutes before she goes," muttered one onlooker, breaking a mesmerized silence.

At precisely 4:49 P.M., the steeple began to teeter. And then, seconds later, down it came, hurtling through the night sky, power lines snapping in unison as it hit the pavement below, exploding on impact. The searing projectile landed in the intersection of Broadway and Pine, where it continued to burn. The hydrant on that corner, which had been relinquished only moments earlier by Engine 18, suffered a direct hit. It was later found to be practically melted.

MORE THAN A HUNDRED firefighters were called to St. Mary's that day. While the fire was declared to be under control by around six P.M., firefighters from the second platoon, including Donny Herbert, stayed on the scene for hours, continuing to pour water on the smoldering rubble so that embers did not reignite and blow over to surrounding homes.

It was a busy shift for Ladder 6, to say the least. From the St. Mary's fire, Donny's ladder truck was then called to the scene of a horrendous automobile accident on the Kensington Expressway that had killed two young Buffalo General nurses. After catching just a few hours of sleep, the platoon awoke to yet another alarm at around six A.M. An electrical fire was torching a one-and-a-half-story frame home on Moselle Street, not too far from another shuttered East Side church, St. Mary of Sorrows. By the time the first firefighters from Ladder 14 arrived on the scene, the house was already half-incinerated. The screams of neighbors told responders that people were trapped inside. The owner of the house, thirty-two-year-old Charles McDaniels, had escaped, but then charged back inside to try to save his wife, Olivia. Now they were both trapped in the bedroom. Two firefighters, Eddie Hughes, from Ladder 14, and Rescue 1's Mike Lombardo, battled their way up the stairs to try to save the two trapped occupants. They were too late. The McDanielses perished, overwhelmed by smoke.

Working a ventilation detail, essentially whacking holes in the windows and sides of the house with an ax, Donny was exhausted, but determined not to let it show. Suddenly, he heard someone shouting to him.

"Hey, give me a hand!" firefighter Lombardo called out the window. He hurriedly instructed Donny to climb up to a porch roof that sat just outside the bedroom window. Lombardo then reached through the window and presented Donny with something heavy. "Here you go," he announced, workmanlike. It was the nude, lifeless body of Olivia McDaniels.

LATER THAT MORNING, Ladder 6 went back over to the St. Mary's scene to help pick up hose, the fireman's equivalent of sweeping up after a party. Everybody pitched in—almost every inch of hose from four battalions had been unfurled to fight this epic blaze. Donny found himself surveying the charred heap of rubble that had once been a marvelous church. Whether a toppled garbage-can fire was the cause, or whether it was something more deliberate, whoever was responsible had done quite a number. The roof had collapsed and the pews and altar were destroyed. Donny was tired, famished. But before he left the scene, he noticed something strange, something he would never forget. Amid the ruin and devastation, all of the stained glass, as well as a majestic marble statue of the Blessed Mother, had somehow survived the fire completely unscathed.

DONNY RETURNED HOME around nine-thirty A.M., bleary-eyed and physically drained. He quietly let himself in the back door, which led into the kitchen. Linda was there making coffee; the kids were still asleep. He reeked of smoke. His hands and face were covered in soot. He appeared to be caught in a daze.

"Geez, you look like you've seen a ghost," Linda said, taken aback by her husband's catatonic demeanor, not to mention the acrid stench of smoke he carried into the house. Linda hadn't heard from Donny since he left the day before, but somehow she had felt certain he would be okay and now was eager to hear about his first time on the job. Donny lit a cigarette and started to detail the night's events, eventually uncorking all the emotions he'd experienced. He held his head in his hands and sighed.

"Lin, I really don't know if I can do this every day."

Hitting him suddenly was the realization that he needed to report back in just another eight hours. Linda had never seen Donny this shaken. She put her arms around him.

"It's okay, Don. You can always go back to your old job," she said, as reassuringly as she could. "You don't have to do this. We'll work it out, okay?"

Later that day Donny did go back to the firehouse. Soon enough he understood that few if any shifts would ever be as eventful as his first. Besides, if there were two qualities about Donny Herbert that were undeniable, they were these: He wasn't afraid of anything, and he *never* gave up.

Two

JUST BELOW THE EASTERN shore of Lake Erie at the mouth of the mighty Niagara River coils the lesser known Buffalo River. A whirlpool of American commerce in the ninteenth century, and for many decades among one of the most polluted rivers in the world, this murky waterway flows west into the lake via a series of loops, up and down, back up and around, ensnaring the city's inner harbor, winding past grain elevators, mills, and factories. Downstream, above the First Ward, near Southside High School, it forks off into Cazenovia Creek. This circuitous tributary, known as "Caz Crick" in South Buffalo, slices dark green through a blue-collar neighborhood, as does Seneca Street, the area's main thoroughfare with which the creek runs parallel. In the 1950s, large sections of the Cazenovia's grassy, oak tree–covered banks were systematically replaced on both sides by enormous concrete slabs, which became known as "the Slants," installed to halt erosion and prevent the flooding of the multitude of wood-frame homes built on both sides of the creek in the crowded parishes of St. Thomas Aquinas and St. Teresa.

Donald Paul Herbert was a pile driver who worked to build the Slants. And he owned one of the homes those barriers were designed to protect. It was a light blue, two-story Cape on Melrose Street, a tidy block of modest homes linking Seneca Street and North Legion Drive, which ran right alongside the Slants. A navy veteran, he was a strong, stocky man who, not unlike a lot of South Buffalo laborers, spent his nonworking hours relaxing with a newspaper in his favorite chair or on a stool at one of the neighborhood's many corner taverns. His wife, Geraldine, drove a school bus. Together they had seven children, four girls and three boys. Their eldest son, born May 7, 1961, was named Donald Joseph. Everyone called him Donny.

From an early age Donny was drawn to Caz Creek, an irresistible siren for any youngster and an endless source of recreation. In the brief but splendid western New York summers, he took full advantage of it, fishing for carp along its banks, swimming in its horseshoe-shaped water-falls upstream, navigating its every winding corner in homemade inner tube rafts. Certain areas were supposed to be off-limits, particularly the ominous stretch buttressed by the dreary gray Slants, just out beyond the Cazenovia Street Bridge where the water was deep and the currents swift. Every few years some poor kid would be fished out of this part of the creek, drowned, although the lingering pall of these seminal tragedies only served to heighten the thrill of braving the forbidden.

Donny's chief partner in exploration was Bobby Bruenn, a husky Melrose kid with a nose for danger. Bobby, who went to Public School No. 27, was six months older and a grade ahead of Donny, who'd started out at nearby St. Teresa's School but transferred to PS 27 after making his first Holy Communion in second grade. Outside the classroom, Donny and Bobby were like a modern-day Tom Sawyer and Huck Finn, spending endless summer days in search of adventure, sometimes even at night when they executed shrewdly planned sneak outs aided by Bobby's strategically favorable garage roof. Their escapades soon exceeded the confines of the creek and the adjacent Caz Park, often landing the brazen duo in dicey situations, whether climbing around the gigantic underground sewer drainage pipes and tunnels that fed into the creek, or hopping aboard freight trains for a quick trip east of the city, where the boys tramped high-grass fields to the back lot of an industrial wire manufacturer that stored heavy-duty coils out back on giant spools. This desolate property afforded the boys their own private jungle gym. Another favorite adventure was closer to home: an undeveloped hideaway of swampy forest and brush piles covering the ruins of an old orphanage. Out here the boys encountered wildlife—pheasants, rabbits, raccoons, and the occasional deer. An early appreciation for the outdoors was encouraged by Bobby's dad, Barney, an insurance salesman who owned a ramshackle clapboard cabin in the woods near the town of Warsaw, New York, forty-five miles southeast of Buffalo. Barney Bruenn often took the two boys out there on weekend hunting and fishing expeditions.

Every April 1, Donny and Bobby skipped school on the occasion of the first day of trout season, hitchhiking south along Old Lake Shore Road, all the way to 18-Mile Creek in Angola, often in freezing cold weather. They didn't necessarily catch much, but they always had a good time.

For one week every July, Donny's family rented a cabin in Letchworth State Park—the "Grand Canyon of the East"—in the highlands south of Rochester. Bobby was always invited to tag along. The two best friends donned cowboy hats and spent hours hiking along and down steep cliffs, some of them as high as six hundred feet. Potential peril abounded in the gorge and along the fast-moving Genesee River, but no one ever got hurt. Donny and Bobby dreamed about one day going out west to see the Rocky Mountains and maybe even the real Grand Canyon.

Donny and Bobby were buddies within a larger pack of intimidating Melrose kids that hung around Seneca Street, clustered on the corner of Seneca and Buffum or in Hillery Playground. In one row of four houses there resided the Herberts, with seven kids; the Bruenn family, who had six children; the Walters family, with seven; and the Potworas, five. In all there must have been at least fifty kids between the ages of seven and fifteen on Melrose Street. Football games, often played on the asphalt street despite the proximity to abundantly grassy Caz Park, were huge happenings, many of them organized by Donny's uncle, a barrel-chested Polish teenager named Simon Manka. Uncle Simon lived a few streets over, on Hammer-schmidt, and was closer in age to his nephew Donny than he was to his sister Geraldine, Donny's mom. Uncle Simon did a lot of babysitting, though as Donny grew older, little of it involved supervision.

Childhood was a time of exceptional freedom for Donny. With his hazel eyes and adorable white blond hair, Donny was his mother's pride and joy. And while his dad could aptly dispense discipline—anyone who ever dared sit in his chair (by the window in the kitchen) could testify to as much—like a lot of men from an older genera-tion, he wasn't big on interacting with his children. When Mr. Herbert put a small aboveground pool in the back-yard, the event was followed by a brief and brutal swim-ming lesson: He threw Donny in. The old man did help coach Little Loop football, along with Simon. Leashing in a daredevil such as Donny would have been impossible anyway.

One spring Saturday Donny and Bobby rode their bikes all the way out to Chestnut Ridge in the leafy, affluent suburb of Orchard Park. A sledding mecca in the wintertime, Chestnut Ridge in the spring was a favorite picnic/party spot, especially among graduating high school seniors. No one would have told them they *couldn't* make it, and if someone had, well, it wouldn't have mattered— their minds were made up, in spite of the fact that Orchard Park, twenty minutes away by car, was a difficult journey for children on scavenged bicycles built from junked parts. Clueless about what they'd bitten off, the twelve-year-old expeditionaries made it there easily enough, traversing a busy thruway overpass and unfamiliar suburban roads.

Soon after arriving, Donny had an idea: They would walk their bikes up to the top of the wooden toboggan run and then ride down. Though it's not clear which of them braved the first trip, both lads wound up with twisted bike frames, flat tires, and enough splinters in their rear ends to last through Labor Day.

AUTUMN REVOLVED AROUND Little Loop football. All of the best young players from the neighborhood were on the prestigious South Buffalo teams, starting with the Saints (nine- and ten-year-olds), the Tigers (ages eleven and twelve), and the Shamrocks (ages thirteen and fourteen). The league had fostered a hearty talent stream feeding the area's best Catholic high school programs. Donny was one of the smallest kids on the field, but with his deceptively muscular frame and fearless attitude, he was possibly the toughest and easily the quickest. The Saints' head coach was a bigger-than-life, jolly fellow named James "Kisty" Riordan, who used Donny at fullback. Big Bobby Bruenn played center. Toughness at twelve was expected, even demanded. Although one day at practice when Bobby hit star running back Larry Potts so hard he broke his team-mate's leg, there was some degree of "dial it down" communicated afterward. With Potts sidelined and his burly best pal blowing open inviting running seams, Donny approached every carry with reckless abandon.

As they got older, aided by their football reputation and zest for excitement, Donny and Bobby emerged as the leaders of their Melrose crew, which included Jimmy Walters, Billy Dietz, and the Potwora brothers, particularly as the gang began to venture into the rough-and-tumble world of Seneca Street after dark. Getting into fistfights was beyond a rite of passage in the neighborhood; it was a regular occurrence, idle entertainment. One prime battleground was in the fields behind the baseball diamonds of Hillery Playground, where large groups of Seneca Street kids waged Friday-night wars over a long, foreboding wooden railroad trestle. Their opponents: a thick congregation of Kaiser-town kids from the other side of the trestle, over in the fields behind Houghton Park. Donny and Bobby fought just about everybody there was to fight. Once in a while they fought each other.

Either because he was rougher around the edges or a little older, Bobby often took the brunt of the blame whenever he and Donny got into trouble. Once when Donny shot out a neighbor's window with a BB gun, it was Bobby who got pinned with the offense. Frustrated, he took it out on his smaller friend, shoving Donny to the ground. As they grappled in the neighbor's driveway, Bobby soon discovered that no matter how hard he pummeled Donny, his foe was unrelenting. The brawl dragged on for more than twenty minutes. When Bobby's older brother finally attempted to separate the two, he found he could not—they were deadlocked in mutual chokeholds. Donny may have taken a few blistering shots that day, but he wasn't licked and he sure as hell wasn't letting go.

BY THE TIME DONNY was ready for high school he'd developed an energetic, industrious streak, instilled in him by his father and his uncle Simon. From the time he could ride a bike, he delivered the *Buffalo Evening News* every day of the week and the free *PennySaver* papers most Saturdays. Donny would spend hours inserting those flimsy classifieds into plastic bags and then much of the day going door-to-door, earning a few cents per every hundred he delivered. Every Sunday night he faithfully took out the garbage for an elderly couple that ran a deli on the corner of Roanoke and Seneca. In the wintertime, he shoveled snow and during the harshest storms dug out drift-entombed automobiles parked along side streets. In the summer he mowed lawns. When he was old enough to drive, he delivered flowers for Foser's Florist. And for a couple of years, Donny worked in his uncle Simon's sub shop. Simon had become a Buffalo cop, and to augment his civil service wages he often undertook side ventures, such as the sub shop (which ultimately closed) and a Laundromat (which later burned down). In the summer months Simon set up a food cart down at the Small Boat Harbor on Lake Erie, selling hamburgers and hot dogs to fishermen. No matter what Simon was up to, Donny was close by, willing to help out.

By the age of sixteen, Donny seemed to be friends with everybody, having broadened his horizons beyond his Seneca Street neighborhood. He began to hang around with kids from all over the area, an ever-expanding network of rowdy friends united by a core group of fifteen or so South Buffalo Shamrock football players. They clung together in their primary stomping ground, Caz Park, despite going to different high schools. Most went to Bishop Timon High School, the largest Catholic all-boys high school in South Buffalo, others to the more academically inclined St. Francis in the lakeside village of Hamburg or to Baker-Victory in the steel city of Lackawanna. Donny went to a public high school, Southside, where his average hovered around 80 percent. For his sophomore year, Donny, on the advice of his parents, transferred to Seneca

Vocational School, where he could learn valuable trade skills such as electronics, and possibly position himself for a career at the power company as a lineman. But Donny was still mostly interested in playing football and having fun with his buddies.

On Friday and Saturday nights, in the dark corners of the vast Cazenovia Park and Golf Course, under bridges and along the banks of the creek, hundreds if not a thousand teenage boys from Timon, St. Franny's, and Baker-Victory hoisted beers and flirted with the Mount Mercy Academy girls. Evenings often ended in either brawls or police raids.

Leaving behind the tradesman track he was on at Seneca Vocational, Donny, at the start of his junior year, transferred to Baker-Victory, named for western New York's most revered spiritual figure, Father Nelson Baker. Donny was recruited by the Fitzpatrick brothers, Paul and Mike, fiery, fiercely competitive coaches who were running an impressive football program at the small coed school, despite losing many of the better, brawnier players to all-boys Timon. The Fitzpatricks more than made do with their collection of little guys. "It doesn't matter how big you are, it's how tough you are," Mike Fitzpatrick would remind them.

The Baker-Victory Braves may have been undersized— Donny Herbert at just five foot seven and 160 pounds was possibly the smallest nose tackle in the history of the

Monsignor Martin Catholic High School Football League—
but they had guts. Donny was considered one of the most
physical players in the league, a literal holy terror on the
gridiron. Quick, powerful, always ready to pop, Donny
unabashedly dictated the fight to his opponents, sometimes
twice his size, and his coaches and teammates loved him
for it. In that season of 1977, with Donny, number 79,
anchoring an impenetrable defense, Baker-Victory went
undefeated, winning the championship of Monsignor Martin's Smith League, a division for small schools. Among the
most unforgettable games that year was played on a Friday
night in steady rain and ankle-deep mud at Lackawanna
Stadium against rival Timon. The Timon Tigers should
have dominated, being part of the other division, the Burke
League, which was for larger schools. However, the out-
come that night was a scoreless tie. Dreadful conditions
aside, and taking into account the David versus Goliath
backdrop, the Baker boys must have trudged out of the
muck-filled trenches with their heads held just a little
higher.

ONE OF DONNY'S CLOSEST friends on the football
team was fellow defensive lineman Mike Faliero, an unas-
suming Italian-American kid from Spaulding Street in St.
Agatha parish. At five foot eleven and 230 pounds, the
mustachioed Faliero was the biggest kid on a Baker-Victory
team brimming with runts. Off the field, Faliero was

ridiculously shy, shunning after-game beer blasts to help out around his father's pizzeria on South Park Avenue. Despite their size difference, Faliero looked to Donny as his protector. Not that he needed one at Baker-Victory.

At most schools, jocks, heads, and nerds usually form distinct groups, and at the very least the graduating twelfth graders indulge seniority. But for some reason, probably because of the small student body's palpable underdog spirit, the four hundred or so boys and girls that filled the halls and classrooms of the crowded two-story, L-shaped building were more like one big happy family. B-V students truly looked out for one another, no matter their differences, from the seniors down to the freshmen. Faculty could sense the special camaraderie and counted it as a blessing.

Many of the students knew, liked, and looked up to Donny Herbert. He was cool. With his shoulder-length dirty blond hair, chiseled good looks, and easygoing way, Donny was the type of kid who never seemed to really know what he had going for him, and if he did, he didn't show it. Guys could share in his glory and not begrudge him. Teachers and coaches appreciated his respectful attitude. Girls found him cute and just plain nice.

A few weeks before Thanksgiving 1977, right after the culmination of the fantastic football season, the students of Baker-Victory were hastily shuffled into the gymnasium for a special morning assembly. They were about to receive some shocking news.

The principal, a well-liked thirty-eight-year-old priest by the name of Father Joseph Penkaul, solemnly announced that the high school would be closing its doors at the end of the following school year. The gym fell completely silent for a few seconds, then erupted with anguished groans and gasps of disbelief.

Exactly why the school was closing—diocesan fiscal straits—didn't matter to the suddenly orphaned students, nor did the wider economic slowdown starting to hit western New York as steel and auto jobs disappeared. All the kids knew was that their much-loved learning institution at 777 Ridge Road was history. Teachers, suddenly facing unemployment, were just as blindsided. One faculty member, a popular gym teacher, Joe Corey, choked up with tears. Others tried to comfort saddened students. A chaotic, emotionally charged scene spilled into the hallways with several students storming out in protest. The end of the line had arrived for a special place.

DURING THE EARLY nineteenth century, not long after the completion of the Erie Canal, what is now the city of Lackawanna was a sprawling reservation of Seneca Indians. The once-proud tribe was thinning in numbers, clustered around picturesque Smoke's Creek and farther north on pristine land formally designated as the Buffalo Creek Indian Reservation under an old colonial charter. The Senecas that remained found themselves ceding increasing amounts of land to religious-minded European settlers such as the Ebenezer Society, a band of German Lutherans. As Buffalo continued to expand into a bustling port city of around twenty thousand people, many of them German and Irish canal laborers, a road was cut to the south directly across the teeming wilderness of the reservation, linking the center of the city to a separate settlement called White Corners. This primitive highway, constructed of wooden planks carved of freshly cut local timber, became known as White's Corners Road. For the most part, the encroaching settlers and the chagrined Senecas worked out their differences peacefully, although most of the Indians pushed farther south, leaving behind a verdant area that rose up into a seedling of a village called Limestone Hill. At some point, around 1850, at the main Limestone Hill intersection of White's Corners and Ridge Roads, a group of Catholic settlers erected St. Patrick's, a minuscule wooden church. It was one of several Roman Catholic churches sprouting up all over nascent Buffalo. St. Pat's wasn't much; it didn't even have a full-time presiding pastor for several years. The first was Reverend Thomas F. Hines, installed in 1857. He also became the head of a newly built home for the growing number of infant children abandoned by destitute parents. The facility was called St. Joseph's Orphan Asylum and was situated next door to the church. Roughly a decade later, Father Hines helped to oversee the completion of a larger orphanage facility for older children. Known as St. John's Protectory, it was a drab, menacing compound replete with iron-bar-clad windows. It housed a hundred or so wayward children dispatched by juvenile courts or forsaken by broken families. This entire complex, known as the Limestone Hill Institutions, became a safe haven for displaced boys who otherwise might have been forced to beg or embark upon criminal pursuits. Father Hines and the nuns who helped him operate this burgeoning "boys town" saw to it that the youth in their care had enough to eat, even if it meant skipping meals themselves. Then, in 1876, Father Hines, getting older and flustered by the financial realities of such ambitious charitable undertakings, took on an assistant, a recently ordained priest who went by the name of Father Nelson Baker.

THE SECOND SON of a German immigrant who owned a general store on the eastern fringe of Buffalo, Baker grew up comfortably, attending public schools and helping out in the family business. After serving in the Union army as a teenager, he marched back to his neighborhood a Civil War hero. It was the summer of 1863 when the young man, seeking to make his own mark, partnered up with an old childhood friend to launch a flour and feed business. Their venture thrived, timed well with Buffalo's boom period. As a leading merchant, highly educated, Baker was well on the road to civic prominence by his midtwenties. One day he happened to stop by the orphanage at Limestone Hill to donate some food and other supplies, something the generous young businessman was prone to do on occasion. Baker had privately contemplated joining the priesthood for some time and confessed as much to Father Hines as they chatted in front of the protectory. The priest suggested that if Baker truly felt that was the path he wanted to pursue, he should visit Bishop Stephen Ryan. Baker did just that. Bishop Ryan in turn offered some stern advice: think it through. During the summer of 1869, racked by indecision but convinced of his calling, Baker, whose father was once a mariner, set out aboard a steamer for a soul-searching journey around the Great Lakes to remote parts of Michigan and Canada, contemplating his future and praying to God for clarity. Not long after his return, Baker stunned his family and friends by announcing that he would be entering Our Lady of Angels Seminary near Niagara Falls. His world, which seemed to be finally coming together, was about to be turned upside down.

While at the seminary, Baker was stricken with a rare, hopelessly fatal disease, erysipelas, or as some called it St. Anthony's Fire. It came without warning and riddled Baker's body with hideous, painful skin lesions, leaving him bedridden for months, totally immobilized. In some two dozen known cases in the Buffalo area, every patient diagnosed with "the fire" had died. Indeed, Baker's death appeared a certainty, so much so that at one point he was given last rites. But right around Easter Sunday of 1872, Baker inexplicably began to recover. Doctors were dumbfounded. His fellow seminarians and priestly instructors, already admiring his courage and resilience, all firmly believed that the former soldier and businessman had been spared by God for a higher purpose.

Not long after getting back on his feet, Baker, while still a seminarian and using his own money, traveled by steamer to France, where he paid a visit to the famous shrine of Our Lady of Victory in Paris. For the spiritual seeker, the pilgrimage was another turning point. He heard the vivid stories of miraculous cures being attributed to prayers at the OLV shrine and about the supposed appearance of the Blessed Mother in nearby Lourdes, France. Upon his return, Baker claimed to have seen firsthand evidence of unexplained healings, and the whole experience seemed to cement his faith.

Nelson Baker was ordained a priest on March 19, 1876. Soon after he took over for Father Hines as pastor of St. Patrick's Church at White's Corners Road in Limestone Hill, which eventually grew into the city of Lackawanna just south of Buffalo. And eventually, Father Baker took charge of the orphanage complex. In one of his first orders, with Bishop Ryan's permission, he changed the name of these institutions to Our Lady of Victory.

Around the turn of the century, more buildings were

added to the Our Lady of Victory community, including elementary and high schools, a massive trade/working school, a new-infants home, a sizable hospital, and in Father Baker's crowning achievement in 1926, the spectacular Basilica of Our Lady of Victory. True to his calling, Father Baker began to display his own brand of bewildering powers. He is said to have cured the sick and dying in numerous instances. While perhaps not technical miracles as sanctioned by the Vatican, many of these occurrences were recorded, including the time he mystifyingly located a natural gas well—a discovery that he attributed to a vision he'd received from the Blessed Mother. This discovery not only blew the minds of the skeptical drilling crew, who were convinced they were engaging in sheer folly, but also those of the citizens of Buffalo and Lackawanna. Meanwhile, the unending supply of fuel helped the OLV Institutions stave off financial crisis and continue to grow. Over the years, more than 300,000 orphaned or troubled "Baker boys" would pass through his care, and most went on to lead productive lives. This remarkable priest, while not officially canonized, was considered to be nothing less than a saint in Lackawanna; indeed, in the entire Buffalo area.

Nearly three decades after Father Baker's death, the historic protectory building, constructed back in 1864 when Lackawanna was still called Limestone Hill, was torn down to significantly enlarge Baker-Victory High School.

For many years Baker-Victory was overshadowed by much larger schools such as all-boys Timon or all-girls Mount Mercy Academy. But by the mid-1970s, Baker-Victory began to emerge as something of a football juggernaut on the coattails of a well-respected basketball program. In fact, in 1977 enrollment was trending up—the fact that B-V was coed was a draw for many pupils, or at least those whose parents were open to the option. Students and faculty were tremendously proud of what their small school's football team had accomplished that autumn. And then just like that, Baker-Victory High School was to be shut down.

Immediately teachers and students began exploring alternatives, even though preparations were being made to accommodate a pared-down class of stragglers who would be allowed to complete the following school year. All sports programs were eliminated. So while Donny and the rest of the returning football players were told they could finish up a lame-duck senior year, without football, few of them considered it for even a minute. All of the former South Buffalo Shamrock players, including Donny, Mike Faliero, Rick Insalaco, Mike Schuster, Kevin Illg, and Billy McCarthy, vowed to stick together no matter what. Soon enough, around Christmas break, they made their decision. Their coaches, the Fitzpatrick brothers, were going their separate ways. Mike Fitzpatrick, who was Baker-Victory's head coach, took a job at St. Francis; his brother Paul was hired to take over the football program at venerable Timon upon the retirement of Coach Joe O'Grady. The Shamrock contingent would follow Paul Fitzpatrick to Timon, right in the heart of their neighborhood.

Donny was now looking at his fourth high school in as many years. He never let on, but it was a tumultuous period for him, his family, and for that matter, Buffalo. The area was still reeling from the disastrous Blizzard of '77 and starting to feel the painful surge of layoffs and recession. Donny's dad found even seasonal construction work hard to come by. The city faced dismal prospects heading into 1978, but someone special was about to come into Donny's life.

ON THE SECOND to last day of 1977, a blustery Friday night, Donny ventured out with some of his old neighborhood buddies, wildman Bobby Bruenn and the equally unpredictable Jimmy Walters. They walked over to a house party given by one of Bobby's best friends from Southside High School. His name was Ray Noe and he lived in the Seneca Babcock section of the city near Republic Steel, a hard-luck area along the Buffalo River where residential streets interwove with chemical plants and fuel storage tanks. Ray Noe's older brother Jimmy had just gotten out of the army, and a lot of friends had been coming by to visit. One of them was Linda Blake.

Linda was a junior at Southside and knew both Ray and Jimmy. A pretty girl with chestnut brown hair parted in the middle, Linda had a friendly way about her and could be quick with a laugh, but at the same time she always kept her guard up. She and Donny started to talk, and soon realized they knew some of the same people. For example, Mike Faliero, Donny's football buddy, had grown up on the same street as Linda, near St. Agatha's Church. She was one of eleven children. Her dad was chief engineer at a public school, her mom a full-time homemaker. Her home, on the corner of Spaulding and Durant, despite being run-down and a bit crowded, was a joyful one. Donny and Linda found they had a lot more in common, and after about an hour they still hadn't run out of things to talk about.

Although Linda wasn't exactly looking for a boyfriend at the time, she did feel she was looking her best in her blue jeans, brown suede boots, and brand-new sweater. She'd babysat for months to save up for that sweater, a white cowl neck purchased at the Seneca Mall. Linda had briefly dated Jimmy Noe, but that was during her freshman year and Jimmy was too old for her. Besides, he was joining the army. They'd stayed friends, though, which turned out to be fortuitous for Donny, who fell right in love with Linda.

The next morning, New Year's Eve day, Linda was more than surprised when Donny Herbert showed up at

her CYO bowling league match at Southside Bowling
Alley. "What the heck are you doing here?" she asked,
almost annoyed but smiling when he played coy. The next
day, Donny, his determination unmasked, stopped by
Linda's house to say hello. "Just passing by," he claimed.
Linda shook her head and, still a little unsure of whether to
be flattered or cautious, suggested they go visit her best
friend, Luanne Schipani, who lived around the corner on
Good Avenue. They spent the afternoon hanging out, listening to Peter Frampton albums. Soon after, Donny and
Linda would hardly ever be apart.

One theory on why Uncle Simon's sub shop failed is
that no one could phone in orders for delivery, because
Donny would call Linda from the shop every night and
they'd talk for hours.

In addition to her babysitting, Linda worked selling
soda and ice cream at Memorial Auditorium when the
Buffalo Sabres were playing at home. She helped Donny
get a concession-stand job right alongside her. On Saturdays, she helped him lug the bundles of *PennySaver*
classifieds that Donny had been delivering door-to-door
since he was in grammar school, until one day he had
enough and flung a full route's worth into Caz Creek. In the
spring, they went to each other's junior proms. By the start
of the summer, they were talking about a future together.

IN LATE JULY Donny started to gear up for Timon football, lifting weights every day at a hole-in-the-wall Seneca Street gym. He was determined to start on defense. During those first August practices at Mulroy Park behind Holy Family Church on South Park Avenue, many of the returning Timon seniors, averse to the foreign infusion and knowing their playing time was threatened, were naturally a little caustic to the Baker-Victory players. Coach Fitzpatrick vowed not to show any favoritism, but despite their lack of size, the Baker kids were better players.

Donny was competing for nose tackle against a returning Timonite and a popular team leader, Billy Goc. During the second week of practice Coach Fitz had Donny and Billy line up mano a mano for a smash-mouth drill. On the final clash Goc, the bigger of the two, slammed Donny to the grass with unmitigated ferocity. Linda and Luanne were nearby watching; Luanne told Donny later she didn't think it was very nice what his teammate had done to him. "Who is that jerk anyway?" Luanne asked. "Oh, that's Billy Goc; he's a good guy," Donny replied. "I don't blame him for knocking me on my ass."

Sure enough, Donny and Billy became fast friends and their alliance helped ease the tension between the Timon and Baker factions. Billy ultimately won the starting nose tackle position, although Donny started right beside him on the defensive line. Placing Donny alongside Goc and quiet strongman Mike Faliero, Coach Fitz had assembled one of the hardest-hitting defensive lines in the Catholic league.

Midway through the season, on October 14, Timon, playing in Lackawanna Stadium, hosted rival St. Francis, in an extra-special grudge match: Coach Paul Fitzpatrick versus Coach Mike Fitzpatrick. But what people most remembered was the incredible play made by Donny Herbert.

It was a damp Saturday evening. Late in the fourth quarter, with Timon leading the mud filled contest 14–0, St. Francis was marching toward Timon's goal line for a touchdown that would put them back in the game. As the St. Francis quarterback turned to deliver a handoff to his running back, Donny scorched through the offensive line with lightning speed, so fast that he stole the ball as the quarterback was delivering it to the running back. Donny Herbert had intercepted *the handoff*.

While Donny was tackled just a few yards upfield, his eye-popping pilfer forcefully reinstated Timon's momentum and left their opponents crestfallen. "I cannot believe you just did that," little Ricky Insalaco gushed on the sidelines. Donny just shrugged his shoulders.

The following week, with a chance to tie untouchable Canisius for a share of the Burke League crown, Timon visited St. Joe's but trailed 21–0 at the half. Coach Fitz delivered a motivational speech in the quiet of the dejected locker room. Put another way: eardrums bled. In the second half, the Tigers scored twenty-three unanswered points and won the game. Timon, fortified by the resilient Baker boys, finished with a tie for the Burke League Championship and its best season in seven years.

Donny graduated from Bishop Timon on Sunday, June 17, 1979. He went right to work as a pile driver. Linda, meanwhile, graduated from Southside around the same time, and got a job working afternoons as a billing clerk for a trucking company near the steel plant. Luanne, two years younger than Linda and still finishing up high school, had started going out with Billy Goc. That summer came the semiscandalous news that Luanne was pregnant. Little Billy junior arrived on a Sunday in February 1980, the same day that the U.S. Olympic hockey team beat Finland to cap off their "Miracle on Ice" gold medal run (best known for the unthinkable upset of the Russians).

A few weeks prior, Donny had gotten a surprise late-night phone call from a buzzed-up Bobby Bruenn. It was a Friday, and Bobby and Jimmy Walters had attempted to have one beer at every tavern on Seneca Street. There were seventeen of them. Stuck at Fibber McGee's and bored with the scenery and dreading the onset of another winter, the boys got to thinking bolder thoughts.

The next day, Saturday, Bobby and Jimmy (and if they could talk him into it, Donny) were going to hitchhike down to Fort Lauderdale, get jobs, and spend the winter basking in the sun. They'd be laughing at their friends back home buried in ice and snow. Dead serious about their plan and uninterested in Donny's stated reluctance, Bobby cajoled his old pal as best he could, but to no avail. Donny, it seemed, had other plans in mind.

Three

DONNY AND LINDA were married on Saturday, January 17, 1981. The weather was bitter cold. A full Roman Catholic ceremonial Mass was held at St. Agatha's Church. Linda's brother-in-law, Jimmy Velasquez, read from Saint Paul's letter to the Corinthians, Chapter 1, verse 13. "In this life we have three lasting qualities—faith, hope, and love," Saint Paul wrote. "But the greatest of these is love."

Donny and Linda listened closely but needed no biblical reminders. They loved each other all right.

A reception was held at the Knights of Columbus hall on South Legion Drive, near Southside High School where Caz Creek forks off into the Buffalo River. Guests looked on, smiling as the couple danced to the first song of the night: "We've Only Just Begun."

Donny had never traveled farther than Letchworth State Park. Linda had been to Florida, to see her cousins in St. Petersburg. That's where these honeymooners were headed. The nineteen-year-olds, sans credit cards and unable to rent a reliable car, set out in Linda's '72 Maverick. They made it as far as a Sheraton Hotel across from the Buffalo Airport before the car began leaking oil.

Donny fixed the oil leak, and on Tuesday, the newly-weds continued on their journey, driving through the afternoon. He was rattled by the rush-hour traffic in Washington, DC, encountered during a spur-of-the-moment side trip to snap a photo of the White House. Linda had hopped out just as President Reagan and a full-blown Secret Service detail were crossing Pennsylvania Avenue following his inauguration. She raced back to the car thrilled to have seen the president and eager to check out a few more tourist sights. Donny, more accustomed to the Buffalo pace, his nerves frayed, issued an executive order: "We're getting the hell out of here."

They drove until Donny got tired and then found a cheap motel. Payoff for one more all-day drive was a fold-out sofa bed at Linda's uncle's house in St. Petersburg. But at least they had made it. Even the morning chaos of Linda's six young cousins getting ready for school as the honey-mooners lay in the middle of the living room didn't bother them—they were together. And, by glory, it was warm!

The rest of their honeymoon was nice; a trip to the ocean, a day at Disney World, visits with the cousins. They made up the itinerary as they went along. The young couple's early years together flowed by in much the same way.

On June 27, 1981, Linda gave birth to their first child, Donald junior. Fourteen months later to the day they had a second son, Thomas. At nearly ten pounds and two feet long, Don junior had been a difficult delivery—the infant's head was misshapen for months from the prying of the doctor's forceps. But Tommy was an even bigger production.

Linda's water broke on a hot August afternoon when she was out strawberry picking with her mother, Mary, and a few of her sisters. Time to go to Mercy Hospital. Donny had been working as a machinist for Delavan Industries, a subsidiary of Ryder on Walden Avenue in Cheektowaga. Delavan manufactured double-decker car haulers for General Motors. Donny was on the second shift, three to eleven, and had carpooled with a Spaulding Street neighbor, Skip Kessler. Linda asked a family friend, Kathy Vonlangen, to drive over to the plant to get Donny and bring him home. As Linda gathered some belongings, Donny made a quick trip over to Mr. Doughnut—but on the way home the car broke down. He fixed it and rushed back to find Linda in a state of panic. By the time they finally arrived at Mercy, Linda was in labor.

Thankfully her sister Sharon was a nurse in the delivery room, because things turned scary pretty quick. The baby had dropped into the birth canal with the umbilical cord wrapped around his neck, not unlike a noose, and it was tightening with every contraction. The doctor, fearing oxygen deprivation and brain damage, ordered an emergency C-section. Tommy would be fine, a healthy nine pounds, ten ounces. Donny named him before Linda was even awake.

A third son, Patrick, came in August of 1984. The family was living in the lower half of an old duplex on Spaulding Street, right across the street from the house in which Linda grew up. Some people would view this as not having gone very far in life, but to the contrary, Linda considered herself lucky. These were carefree days. Donny was making a decent salary and earning extra money in the warmer months helping out Bobby Bruenn with his roofing and siding business.

Right down the street, on Good Avenue near St. Agatha's, lived Luanne and Billy, who had moved into Luanne's childhood home with their three kids. Another close friend, Terri Drilling, had gotten married and also bought her family's home on nearby Lilac Street.

Many of the girls who once played together in St. Agatha's Parish were now raising families of their own here. One neighborhood girl, Norberta Duringer, orphaned as a teenager along with a houseful of younger siblings, one of whom was Linda's close friend Althea, had practically been raising a family from the time she was a junior in high school. Linda always felt bad for Berta, who was forced to grow up in a hurry.

Donny and Linda's home on Spaulding was full of warmth and activity. Mainly it was just full, with kids, toys, cousins, and neighborhood kids. In the backyard, Donny ran a virtual animal shelter. There were ducks, rabbits, turtles, cats, and the occasional stray dog. Eventually, the family did get a dog of their own, a free-roaming mixed breed named Shorty. Luckily, their landlady, who lived upstairs, did not mind the Spaulding zoo. She was an elderly widow, Bessie Cummings, painfully arthritic and frail, though endlessly kind. Donny and Linda always felt for her. She had had a tough life. Her first husband had been a drunkard and abusive. Her second husband died of a stroke. A daughter had died in her twenties of a brain tumor, and her son-in-law had moved far away with the grandchildren. But Bessie's heart had already been irreparably shattered many, many years earlier when her precious little two-year-old boy was killed before her eyes, stumbling into a tub of lye used for handmade laundry detergent. The toddler was burned alive. Bessie still kept his little baby shoes, which she'd had bronzed, hanging over the fireplace. Donny always made sure Bessie had a ride to the grocery store or to the doctor, sometimes gently (just as often impatiently) carrying her down the stairs. If anything needed fixing, he was always there to help.

Much of South Buffalo could have said that about Donny Herbert. A few years of working as a roofer and contractor had turned Donny, his forearms already Popeye-cut from pile driving, into a first-rate handyman. His inability to ever say no led to repairs and projects all over the neighborhood, usually for a few extra bucks, sometimes for no charge at all.

Donny wasn't thrilled with his job at Delavan, though he always put forth his best effort. As machinists went, he was one of the more precise of the lot. The plant was a dingy, oppressive environment, where, on any given day, Donny would spend eight hours on one of two dozen machines, fabricating one of the hundreds of parts that went into making trailers. Delavan assembled the rigs right there at the part-making plant, one at a time, from start to finish. The days were long; only two crisp ten-minute breaks and a half hour for lunch were allowed. The work itself often involved the same activity, over and over. It could also be dangerous work. Machinists often had their hands and fingers smashed or sliced by clamps and drills, or burned by tolvene solvent in which the parts were dipped to attain that metallic sheen. Linda's uncle, Pete Terzian, was the plant manager. He'd gotten Donny the job, which paid about twelve dollars an hour. A lot of guys were grateful to have the job, grind that it was. More than a thousand Republic steel workers, including Donny's neighbor Skip Kessler, had just been laid off with the plant closing, and a lot of them had come to Pete Terzian for work as welders and machinists. He accommodated as many as he could.

Kessler was a bear of a guy in his late thirties and he'd spent the decade of the seventies catching red-hot, oven-belched steel bars with a set of heavy tongs. He was the unofficial sheriff of Spaulding Street. When there was commotion in the neighborhood, it was Skip Kessler, and not the police, whom people called. He drove Donny to and from work every day so that Linda could use the Chevette. Sometimes on the way home, Donny would light a smoke, lean against the window, and lament the machinist's life. "I gotta get out of here," he'd say. Kessler either laughed or said nothing at all, but never argued the point.

A few times a week during the winter Donny worked an overnight detail for Linda's dad, chief engineer at PS 74 on the East Side. Donny's task was to fire up the boilers so the classrooms would be warm in the morning. He did a bit of sweeping, took out some garbage, but for the most part it required little effort. He passed the time listening to 97 Rock, Buffalo's classic rock station, or racking out on an army surplus cot. Donny split his side job with a carrot-topped North Buffalo bartender named Jimmy Seemueller, who was married to Linda's younger sister Mary.

Jimmy was a disillusioned Canisius College graduate whose father had just died. He'd dreaded the expected white-collar sales and marketing track for which his business degree positioned him. The truth was he had never wanted to do anything but become a Buffalo firefighter. Jimmy ended up toiling away at the U.S. Sugar refinery plant on Bailey Avenue as a quality inspector, and ultimately found civil service employment at City Hall as an adjuster in the water department. One day in the winter of 1985, Jimmy heard word trickle down that the fire department was going to embark on a seminal recruiting campaign, lining up three classes for more than a hundred slots. The first step was a written test; a date was set, but it had not yet been announced to the public.

"You know, Donny, you ought to consider taking the test," Jimmy told his brother-in-law a few weeks later during a family gathering. He knew how badly Donny wanted to get out of Delavan. Donny was all ears.

"I really think it's a perfect job for a family man like yourself," Jimmy explained. "With those four days off in a row, you'd be able to spend a lot of real quality time with your kids, and plus, you're in good shape."

Donny had never contemplated joining the fire department before, but on Jimmy's advice, he took the written test and passed. A few months later it came time for the physical, a seven-event gauntlet that included an obstacle course, pylon sprints, a dummy drag, a tunnel crawl, and most taxing of all, a five-flight stair climb carrying fifty pounds of hose. Donny crushed it. When the candidates list came out in the summer of 1986, Donny was number twenty, giving him a spot in the next class, which would convene in October. Jimmy Seemueller, still working in the water department at City Hall, caught an early leak of the list and who'd placed where. Jimmy wound up farther down and had to wait two years for his class, but he was excited at least to have made it. He rushed to Spaulding Street to deliver the good news. Skip Kessler had just dropped Donny off after another grueling day at the plant.

"Donny!" Jimmy called to him from his car. "The list comes out tomorrow—you're number twenty. You're in the first class!"

Donny broke out in an ear-to-ear grin. His Delavan days were officially numbered. "Finally," he said.

DONNY JOINED THE FIRE DEPARTMENT at a time when a lot of the old-timers were retiring amid a push for more blacks and women. Plenty of spots were doled out in the neighborhood. Mayor Jimmy Griffin lived in South Buffalo. The two-month training program at the academy in Cheektowaga began on October 20, 1986. The classes ran from Monday through Friday, eight A.M. to five P.M. Donny enjoyed the mix of physical training and classroom sessions, but the best part was the simulations out at the "smoke house." By all accounts, Donny was considered among the very best of the forty-some-odd candidates. He was gung-ho all right. One Saturday Donny even staged an ad hoc fire safety exercise in the attic on Spaulding, blind-folding Don junior and Tommy with bandannas and teaching them how to crawl out, just as he'd learned during training courses.

The swearing-in ceremony was held at the academy on Thursday, December 18; nothing too fancy, but a few hundred people were on hand, seated in long rows of wooden folding chairs. Linda had dressed the boys up in sweaters, corduroys, and shiny shoes. When Donny's name was called and he was presented with his certificate of achievement recognizing completion of the training course, Linda and the kids clapped loud and long. Later on, as Linda was shuffling outside with the boys, a paunchy, gray-haired priest approached her.

"Hello. I'm Father Al Clody," he said. "I'm the fire department chaplain."

"Oh, hello," Linda replied.

"I just wanted to introduce myself," Father Clody said. "If there's ever anything I can do for you, please don't hesitate to ask, okay?"

Corralling the children as best as she could, Linda turned and gave the priest a friendly glance of mild exasperation. She knew of the fire department chaplain. When a fireman is injured or worse, it was Father Clody who knocked on your door.

"Well, it was nice meeting you, Father," Linda said with the start of a chuckle. "And no offense, but I hope I never meet you again."

MOST OF THE GUYS working second platoon on Ladder 6/Engine 21 were brand-new firefighters. With so much inexperience, there were the occasional screwups, such as the time a rookie from Donny's class named Tony Serafini backed the ladder truck straight into a wooden staircase, completely taking it out.

As rookies went, Donny was neither overwhelmed nor overconfident, treating each call with an unwavering attention to doing the job well. Some firefighters, especially the older guys, might have preferred an uneventful tour, but not Donny. He usually sat in the kitchen, caffeinating, smoking Marlboro menthols, drumming his fingers on the table, anxious to hear the three long loud beeps that preceded a dispatch of a working structure fire. To blow off steam, Donny played handball upstairs, or did push-ups and sit-ups. His old pal Bobby Bruenn had recently introduced him to bow hunting, so sometimes Donny would spend downtime treating himself to some target practice out back. Normally Donny slept only five or six hours a night, and in the mornings when he returned home to Linda and the kids, he was more than happy to fix breakfast, fold laundry, or help clean around the house. He was always doing something with the kids: camping, fishing, sledding, coaching T-ball. Luanne and Terri would often joke with Linda over coffee that she should bottle some of Donny's blood and sell it to some of the wives in the neighborhood to give to their husbands. They all knew Donny was one of a kind, and that unlike many young South Buffalo men, his entire life revolved around taking care of his family.

Money was tight, and life was never easy, but days unfolded slowly, simply. While they saved what they could,

Donny and Linda never looked too far ahead. All that summer of 1987 the family spent nearly every weekend at Arrowhead Campground, an hour south of Buffalo. The owners, the Bull family, loved Donny and always reserved for him the most secluded spot. Luanne, Billy, and their kids would also join in. Sometimes Donny would drive everyone out in the morning, set up camp, pitch tents, chop firewood, and then drive back to the city to work overnight at the firehouse, returning the next morning to make breakfast and take all the kids fishing. Donny always made sure they had working poles and that their hooks were baited.

One August Donny and Linda loaded up their hatchback and took the kids to Disney World. With his family crammed into the car and sunny skies before him, Donny pulled into the corner gas station as hyperexcited as his young boys, all tucked in the backseat with their toys and a coolerful of treats. He cherished the idea of taking his family on their first real vacation together and could not wait for the smiles when they arrived at the gates of the Magic Kingdom. Clad in a T-shirt and swimming trunks, Donny was already in the Florida spirit as he paid for the gas. He'd ordered a large cup of coffee to fuel the first leg of their journey. That would turn out to be a mistake. Only one minute into the trip Donny stopped abruptly at a red light, spilling the scalding coffee all over his lap. Screaming bloody murder, he floored it, heading over to his mother's house on Melrose for a badly needed ice pack and a new pair of shorts. Once back on the road, somewhere near the first toll booth, Patrick got carsick and threw up all over the backseat. Donny pulled off to the side to do a fast cleanup. The Herberts had made it a whole three miles.

Eventually the family did make it to Disney World, stopping first for a few days at Uncle John and Aunt Kay's in St. Pete. On his honeymoon, Donny had seen the ocean for the first time, but he had not actually ventured in for a swim. This time he would. And while Disney World was a blast, it was on Cocoa Beach a few days before they were set to head back that Donny reached vacation nirvana. Frolicking in the waves with Linda and the boys, Donny, wearing a silly, oversized Batman tank top Tommy had picked out for him for Father's Day, was one happy man. He'd realized that despite the rocky start, his first real family vacation had been a complete success.

"This was a great trip," Donny declared to Linda as they loaded up for the long drive back to Buffalo. "It sure was," Linda replied with a nervous laugh. Donny knew exactly what she was thinking: All they had to do was make it home.

JUST AFTER THANKSGIVING, DONNY AND LINDA attended the funeral of a friend's husband. Debbie Benedick was Linda's classmate at Southside High School. She, too, had been married young, to a friendly Cheektowaga kid named Dave Strzalkowski. Dave's dream was to become a police officer. Too short to qualify for the Buffalo Police Department, he was able to qualify for the Metro-Dade Police Department. After six years on the force, Officer Strzalkowski, responding to a report of a domestic dispute, was shot to death by a recently released felon. A funeral was eventually held in Buffalo, at which time his inconsolable young widow was formally presented with a ceremonial American flag.

During the car ride home, Linda couldn't escape the image of Debbie holding the flag. She couldn't imagine what she would do if anything ever happened to Donny. "I don't know how Debbie is going to make it through this," Linda said, sniffling. "It's so awful."

Donny drove in silence. Since he'd entered the fire department there had been no real discussion of the danger inherent in his job, but it came up now: "Don't you expect me to hold any flag!" Linda yelled to her husband with a mixture of frustration and fury. "You got that?!"

"Lin, come on," Donny said.

"No way," Linda huffed, cementing her point. "I'm not going to do it."

IN OCTOBER OF 1987 Pope John Paul II, in conjunction with the sacred Congregation for the Causes of the Saints at the Vatican, delivered exciting news to the Catholic Diocese of Buffalo. Its request to start the process of canonization for Monsignor Nelson H. Baker had been granted. In the first official step of three on the road to sainthood, and almost more of a formality, Father Baker, who'd been called "Padre of the Poor" in life, was posthumously bestowed the title of "Servant of God." Going forward, to get to stage two, beatification, an excruciatingly detailed investigation into Father Baker's life and works would need to take place, including the rigorous verification from church authorities in Rome that a miracle—something otherwise inexplicable either naturally or scientifically—had occurred because someone prayed for Father Baker's intercession.

Monsignor Robert C. Wurtz was carrying on the Baker legacy as head of the Our Lady of Victory institutions. As such, it would be Wurtz who would lead the canonization effort. Wurtz had his work cut out for him. At the same time he had a multitude of stirring examples from which to choose, with more unbelievable stories of Father Baker's healings coming in every day. Most involved a hopelessly desperate medical crisis resolved with no other explanation than prayers to Father Baker, either at the basilica shrine or upon a blessed cross or a piece of the iconic priest's clothing. Stories started to pour in from all over western New York, some from people who previously had never revealed the episodes but decided to come forward to help Baker's case for sainthood. Down the road, evidence of a second miracle would be required. For a miraculous claim to pass

Vatican muster, Wurtz would need proof that it could not otherwise be naturally or medically explained, and that it happened solely through the divine intercession of Father Baker. It had taken five decades for the sainthood cause to even get this far. The most arduous phase was only beginning.

Four

A REAL ESTATE AGENT knocked on the Herberts'
door one day and explained to Linda that her landlady, Bessie Cummings, wanted to sell them the house at
90 Spaulding for fifteen thousand dollars. Considering the
fact that the property could have sold for twice that
amount, this was the equivalent of Donny and Linda's
hitting the lottery. But old Bessie had two conditions. The
first was that she could live there, upstairs, until she died.
Second, she insisted on paying rent, $150 a month, which
worked out to be exactly the monthly mortgage payment.

The following spring Donny bid for a slot on Engine 3,
paired with Rescue 1 in a firehouse built in 1981 on the
corner of Broadway and Monroe in yet another East Side
ghetto. Only sixteen months on the job, Donny one day
hoped to make it on the Rescue—one of the busiest crews
in the department—after he'd gained some more seniority.

With her three boys attending St. Agatha's grammar
school, Linda took a part-time job as a secretary at RAF
Supply Inc., a tool-making company near the steel plant.

Every now and again on Father's Day or near Donny's birthday she brought Donny a big bag of stainless-steel screws and, one time, a brand-new cordless power drill her boss let her have for free.

Life's simple joys did not go underappreciated in the Herbert household. The family enjoyed spending time together, whether walking the trails of Tifft Nature Preserve or going out for breakfast after ten o'clock Mass on Sunday. Though certainly not Bible thumpers, Donny and Linda were both committed to being good, practicing Catholics and wanted the same for their boys.

In May of 1990, Don junior made his first Holy Communion. Donny glowed with satisfaction. The following May, Tommy made his, and Donny was just as proud. They had some party that day. Linda's sister Sharon finagled a pony for the afternoon—right in the front yard—and Donny made sure that every little kid in the neighborhood got a ride.

The three Herbert boys were tight, constantly playing together as three best friends, but in just a few short years each had come into his own. The eldest, Don junior, and Tommy were particularly close at just fourteen months apart, both of them cheerful and outgoing. Tommy was the natural athlete, Don junior a straight-A student. The youngest, Patrick, was more on the shy side and a little chubby. But he, too, had his dad's competitive streak and could certainly hold his own on the soccer field.

Donny and Linda kept the house at 90 Spaulding, renting out both the upstairs and downstairs. Meanwhile, they purchased a small, bargain fixer-upper right around the corner, on Sirrett Street. Both floors were theirs and theirs alone. However, by the late spring of 1991, Linda was expecting their fourth child. Even with those second-floor bedrooms, space would be an issue.

One day that summer, after Linda had dropped Donny off at the firehouse, she happened to drive by some pretty, new houses in an otherwise dingy stretch of the East Side. She'd read in the newspaper about these homes, built through a Housing and Urban Development loan program.

For years, Linda casually had her eye on nearby Durant Street, a desolate cut-through road of weed-strewn vacant lots that bisected the warehouses and trucking companies of Hopkins Street from busy South Park Avenue. To most people in the parish, Durant was an eyesore. Linda always thought it could easily be cleaned up. On a hunch, she phoned the office of Brian Higgins, a preppy thirtysomething councilman representing the city's south side, to inquire about the Durant Street lots. The response from Higgins's secretary a few days later was, surprisingly, yes, the lots on Durant Street were owned by the city. And moreover, yes, the Herberts qualified for a twenty-thousand-dollar HUD grant, and yes, they could build there.

That summer, contractors, with Donny supervising

every step of the way, began laying the foundation and frame of the very first house on Durant Street. Others would soon follow. The Herberts' small home was erected exactly to government specs, but once they were legally the owners, they were free to make changes as they pleased. The family moved into their new home just before Labor Day. Immediately, Donny began to renovate and plot an expansion. He'd framed an upstairs bedroom by the end of their first weekend. Within a month, Donny had the addition finished. By Thanksgiving, he had turned the tiny garage into a family room. His next project would be another bedroom, plus a new family room, though these would have to wait for the spring.

One weekend, a couple of weeks before Christmas 1991, Buffalo was walloped by a winter storm that brought almost a foot of snow. Linda was six weeks from her delivery date, which for her could not come soon enough. Three babies in four years had not been easy, but Linda had been in her early twenties and never found the actual pregnancies to be burdensome. She and Donny hadn't done much in the way of family planning in the early days. Now, with the three boys shooting up so fast and seven years having gone by since their last baby, they were keen on having one more. But this time Linda was nearly thirty years old, and every day brought nausea, fatigue, and as the pregnancy wore on and on, an overriding state of misery. Donny could not make her feel better, try as he might to keep her spirits up.

On this particular Sunday, Donny was fretting over the flat roof on the converted-garage living room. He became convinced that it was covered with too much snow and could cave in easily, or at the very least cause water damage. Linda understood what he was contemplating and threw her hands up as she exclaimed, "Whoa, whoa, wait a minute. You're not going up on the roof, are you?"

"It's no problem. I'm just going to shovel the snow off of there—I'll be fine."

No, Linda insisted. She was adamant. This was a bad idea.

"Don, come on. It's windy, it's icy, I'm seven months pregnant with three young kids, and you know the last thing I need is for you to fall off the roof and break your neck. Please don't!"

But Donny was always a stubborn fellow, and so he got out the ladder, all the while assuring Linda nothing bad was going to happen. A few minutes later as Linda was folding some laundry, she heard a loud thud, followed by a groan. Tommy and Patrick, playing in the snow in the front yard, came running in the house in a panic.

"Mommy, Mommy, Daddy fell off the roof!"

Linda did not even look up. At that moment she was more angry than worried. Outside, Donny was in a heap on the icy sidewalk near the front steps.

"Is he alive?" Linda asked in a blasé monotone.

The boys nodded that indeed he was.

"Well, is he hurt?"

They ran outside to check.

"Daddy, are you okay?"

Donny, just getting to his feet, informed them that indeed he was, but truth be told, he'd had the wind knocked out of him and could barely stand. Later, embarrassed, back stiff, and moving at a pace worthy of Bessie Cummings, Donny tiptoed back into the house. Linda was at the kitchen sink peacefully doing the dishes, still a tad sore herself. *She'd begged him.*

"Weren't you even going to come check to see if I was okay?" Donny asked, sheepishly looking down.

Linda could not stay mad at Donny and gave him an affectionate smile.

"Yeah, I guess eventually I would have come out to check on you. But the kids said you were all right."

She checked his injuries and ran a tub for him. Donny's entire body was black-and-blue. That night over dinner, the whole family had a hearty laugh over Dad's classic one-liner to Patrick after the child had asked if he was okay.

"I'm fine—the concrete broke my fall."

ABOUT TWO WEEKS LATER, Linda was the one who proved to be overly obstinate. It was December 23, and a Christmas-present-wrapping session was planned at her younger sister Jean's house two blocks away. Nearly all of Linda's ten siblings owned or rented in St. Agatha Parish or within a mile of their family house at 77 Spaulding. Linda, despite being warned to stay off her feet as her due date approached, had loaded up the trunk of her car with several large plastic bags filled with toys, even lugging a heavy aluminum pole that was part of a mini basketball set for the boys. She might have thrown her back out in the process, but somehow she managed to get all of the presents over to Jean's, wrap them, and then load them back into her car.

As Linda started home, she thought she felt her water break. Donny had just finished mopping the ceramic kitchen floor and was doing dishes when Linda came flying through the side door, heading straight for the bathroom.

"Hey, be careful," Donny called out. "The floor's still—"

Linda cut him off as she rushed by. "My water broke!"

They called the doctor, gathered up some things in the station wagon, brought the kids down the street to Linda's parents, and sped over to Children's Hospital, their dog, Shorty, chasing behind them for as long as he could keep up.

When they arrived at the hospital Linda was admitted immediately, though only as a precaution. Her water had not actually broken, but she was leaking amniotic fluid.

"But tomorrow is Christmas Eve," she protested,

although her obstetrician was unmoved. The next day was filled with X-rays and tests, and Linda was still leaking fluid. That evening, Donny took the boys to church and over to his parents' house on Melrose, and then over to Linda's parents' on Spaulding, which on Christmas Eve was so overrun with giddy, Santa-stoked grandchildren that the hardwood floor became a fluid cluster of wrapping paper, shrieking giggles, and flying pajamas. Later that night, sitting on the couch watching one of his two all-time favorite movies, *It's a Wonderful Life* (the other was *Blazing Saddles*), Donny phoned the hospital to find Linda in a state of woe. Not only was she missing Christmas, but she was also in a lot of pain. Over the phone, Linda could hear the children laughing excitedly, and it made her all the more depressed.

The next morning Donny and the kids came back to the hospital to visit her.

"Merry Christmas!" Donny proclaimed, handing Linda a present to unwrap.

"A hair dryer?"

It wasn't that Linda didn't like hair dryers or this particular model. It was just that they each strived to live as frugally as possible. The point was, she already had a hair dryer.

"Well, I figured, you know, since we have two bathrooms now, you could keep a hair dryer in each one," Donny explained.

"Good idea," Linda said, her emotions suddenly swinging wildly. Touched by the gesture, she reached out for a hug. "Thanks, hon, I love it."

TWO DAYS LATER on December 27, 1991, Linda gave birth to a fourth son, Nicholas Ryan Joseph. More than a month premature, oxygen starved, severely jaundiced, and a mere peanut of a human form, Nicholas nevertheless weighed a respectable five pounds. But he had to fight through his first few days on Earth sleeping in an incubator. When he was finally removed, Donny joked that the newborn looked like one of the kids' "glow worm" toys, but as the fourth-time dad made this comment, the expression on his face was one of nervous relief following several days of racking uncertainty, and not smug sarcasm. But Nicky was not out of the woods just yet.

About a month later, the poor baby boy, lungs underdeveloped, fell ill with pneumonia and for a spell appeared to have trouble breathing. Donny and Linda jumped into the station wagon to drive the sick boy to their family doctor in Orchard Park. Shorty chased along the whole way. As soon as the doctor saw the boy, he immediately called 911. Minutes later, some volunteer firemen and an ambulance arrived. Nicky, his every breath growing frighteningly more shallow, was rushed to Children's Hospital, Linda by his side in the ambulance. Donny followed right behind in the wagon. Despite the scare, Nicky would be okay. However, poor Shorty, perhaps disoriented after losing his owners' scent in the ritzy outer suburbs, never returned home again. The boys—and most of all, Linda—were heartbroken. For years they searched for their dog and held out hope that by some fluke he would be found. But he never was.

WITH THE OLDER KIDS at school, Donny, off for four days in a row between tours at the firehouse, was delighted to have Nicky to buddy around with. Linda was home all day, too. These were some difficult times for her. She found herself battling depression and crippling anxiety, the whole time gaining weight, which only exacerbated the problem. Donny, often feeling the brunt of Linda's outbursts, grew frustrated because it seemed there was nothing he could do to make her happy. Linda, confused and feeling helpless to do anything about her worsening condition, often retreated to the couch, sleeping the day away in a weary funk. But through it all, no matter how stressful things got, each showed a willingness and determination to somehow work it out. Linda eventually sought treatment for her tumultuous mental state, which was diagnosed as postpartum depression.

If things at home weren't picture-perfect, Donny's career with the fire department was going exceptionally well. He made it on Rescue 1, which had been his goal.

Rescue was the place to be for aggressive firefighters, guys who really loved the action. The two rescue companies, 1 and 2, split the entire city, responding to every structure fire, car crash, or any other accident involving reports of injuries. Due to city budget cuts, Rescue 2 would eventually be eliminated altogether, leaving Rescue 1 to be at the entire city's beck and call. Not surprisingly in a struggling economy, arson became an epidemic. That, coupled with a high percentage of old, wooden homes relative to most cities its size, meant Buffalo had one of the busiest fire departments in the country. Despite the workload, Donny and the rest of the guys never complained. There rarely was a dull moment, and the pace suited them just fine.

His new gang on the second platoon became something of an extended family. Among his best friends at the firehouse were Gary O'Neill, a fellow South Buffalonian with whom Donny often carpooled to work; Jerry Johnson, one of only a handful of black firefighters to make it to the rescue company; and burly Mike Lombardo, who years earlier had introduced himself to Donny by handing him the deceased smoke-inhalation victim. Lombardo, who had lost his dad at an early age, had practically been raised in a Colvin Avenue firehouse, where he used to hang around like a stray cat. Lombardo was not the only hard core assigned to Rescue Company 1. There were older guys, true fire buffs like Paddy "Cuddles" Coghlan, who kept an emergency band radio in every room of his house and who, when not fighting fires, drove around the city taking photographs of them. Then there was John Breier, who drove the Rescue 1 rig despite having suffered hearing loss in both ears after a tragic December 1983 propane explosion that took out an entire city block, killing five firefighters.

Breier and "Herby," as he called Donny, often stayed up late at night in the kitchen, sipping coffee together, talking about life, family, kids, pressure, whatever was on their minds. With double hearing aids cranked on high and a fatherly way about him, old Johnny Breier was acutely skilled in the art of listening.

Another "buff" and semifixture at the firehouse was a gregarious young Catholic priest by the name of Father Joe Bayne, a Baltimore native whose firefighter dad had been killed in the line of duty. In addition to running a youth shelter on Seneca Street and saying the occasional mass at St. Agatha's, Father Joe served as chaplain for Erie County Emergency Services. He also helped out Monsignor Clody, the BFD chaplain. Father Joe, who like Mike Lombardo practically grew up in a firehouse, enjoyed riding along with Donny on Rescue 1, and the two of them became close friends. Donny also got to know another Father Joe, Father Joseph Moreno, the chaplain for the Buffalo Police Department. Roly-poly, bushy-haired Father

Joe Moreno, like Donny, went to virtually every tragic accident scene in the city, blessing critically injured victims.

When calls were slow and the walls of the firehouse seemed as if they were closing in, Donny would organize spirited volleyball games out back, or intensely competitive—at times downright savage—two-on-two hockey games in the narrow hallway outside the bunk room, sometimes leaving windows and egos shattered, such was Donny's competitive zeal. He played to win. He fought fires the same way. In dangerous situations, Donny could be brash—always the first one to rush in—but he wasn't out for glory.

One early spring evening, a few days before the annual Buffalo Fire Department Ball, Donny found himself swilling a few cold beers with childhood pal Bobby Bruenn. Donny was explaining that the department was giving out awards to around twenty-five firefighters for acts of bravery and that he would be one of them. Specifically, Donny was getting the Marine Corps League Award for dashing into a burning Jefferson Avenue apartment to retrieve two small children, tucking each one under his powerful arms like spare umbrellas, and delivering them to safety. He then crawled back into the smoke-filled apartment and carried out a twenty-five-year-old woman. The story as Donny told it—although he wasn't really bragging—sounded harrowingly badass to Bobby. Not to Donny. He'd only mentioned it to underscore his discomfort about getting the award. Anybody would have done what he had done given the circumstances.

"Come on, Donny, how many people can say that they saved a human life?" Bobby asked. "Shit, three of 'em!"

Donny had taken part in many rescues. There were people who walked the earth only because he had been there to save them. Donny's reputation around the fire department was that of someone with a unique passion for the job. But being a fireman was not his life; he lived for Linda and the kids.

Finishing off a can of Genesee beer, Donny countered Bobby with a shrug. "I just don't see the point of giving me an award. It's my job. I like it. They pay me to do it. That's enough."

Bobby just laughed. Man, could his old pal be stubborn.

ONE MORNING IN late May of 1994, Donny was in the backyard hammering together a flower bed for Linda. He loved to work around the yard, shirt off, ball cap turned backward, Creedence Clearwater Revival blasting from a duct-taped boom box.

As Donny went about his work, little Nicky, bored with his Tonkas, had to know: What was his dad doing that could possibly make such a clatter?

"Stay back," Donny told him firmly, then for a second time.

But Nicky, not yet three, didn't listen. He inched closer to peer at the ongoing carpentry project. Too close.

In a swift, split-second moment, Donny swung the hammer back and accidentally whacked the overly curious child with the V-shaped claw. He'd struck the toddler right between the eyes.

Nicky let out a piercing shriek, blood gushing down his face. Donny, who as a firefighter assigned to Rescue 1 often went from one gruesome accident to the next, flew into an outright panic. He could hardly bear to look at Nicky's face as he rushed the boy into the house.

"Linda!" he screamed, grabbing a washcloth.

Bursting into tears, Donny told Linda what had happened. Another inch could have maimed or even killed the child. He still couldn't look. Linda took a glimpse. The boy's eyes and nose looked undamaged to her, but there was a lot of blood.

Normally, Linda would have been the one freaking out. She was surprised Donny was so fraught but understood.

Okay, I have to be the one in control.

Linda put Nicky in the front seat and urged Donny, still teary eyed and profusely apologizing to his son, to calm down as he started the wagon. They rushed Nicky to Mercy Hospital two minutes away. Doctors were amazed that the injury wasn't worse; just two stitches.

Nicky took them like a man. And he was even proud

afterward, telling his brothers to check out his "whack in the head."

Poor Donny never fully got over it.

IN THE AUTUMN of 1994, Bessie Cummings, too ill to live alone and on the prompting of a grandchild who had returned to the area, begrudgingly went into a nursing home. Though they still checked in on her every so often, Donny and Linda didn't realize until a week or so later that Bessie had moved out of the house at 90 Spaulding. Linda felt terrible.

Bessie had been a major part of their lives. She wanted to go visit her, but wasn't sure where Bessie was. Linda eventually tracked her down after calling around to nursing homes in the vicinity. At an overcrowded facility north of Buffalo, Linda found Bessie only partially alert. The next time Linda went to see her, a few weeks later, Bessie was completely incoherent—motionless, lying on her side, mouth agape, gripped by a sleepy stupor. Linda never saw Bessie again. She died a few weeks later.

THE FOLLOWING SUMMER, Linda's aunt Ellen, a lovable, bighearted woman, called Donny to put in new gutters. Ellen, her husband, Jim, who worked for Ford, and their kids lived out in Orchard Park, near Chestnut Ridge. Donny was off that day from the fire department and told her he would be happy to help. When he arrived, Ellen mentioned that she had noticed some water damage on the ceiling. She assumed the old, clogged gutters were the culprit but her handyman had a different theory on the source of the leak.

"I'll go check the attic," Donny said.

"You sure you want to go crawling around in there?" Aunt Ellen asked as she poured Donny a cup of coffee.

"No problem; I do it all the time," Donny replied.

One thing about Donny—he loved coffee, especially the endless supply found over at Linda's mom's house, on the stove, in the old heavy metal percolator. Aunt Ellen made a good cup, too.

"Just last week I got stuck in an attic during a fire," Donny continued nonchalantly.

"Oh, my God, Donny," Aunt Ellen gasped. "Weren't you scared?"

"Nah," he scoffed with a big smile. "I knew one of my guys would come get me. Hey, don't tell Linda about that, okay? I wouldn't want to worry her."

"Sure, Don," she replied. "I won't say anything."

Aunt Ellen kept her word.

ON A SUNNY MORNING in October of 1995, Donny Herbert exited the back door of the firehouse and climbed into his secondhand Chevy Caprice station wagon. The unusually warm Indian summer weather instilled a sense of contentedness as he pulled out of the parking lot, headed for home.

The Herbert residence on Durant Street had come together quite nicely, and of course Donny was still expanding and improving. He had even put in an aboveground pool—single-handedly—one section at a time, a mind-bending task requiring immeasurable patience, not to mention a bottomless supply of screws. The pool, rectangular with five-foot sides and a wraparound deck, looked brand-new, but it was actually used. Donny had agreed to tear it down for one of the dads on Tommy's soccer team. In the dismantling process, Donny coded every single piece with a permanent Magic Marker and loaded them all in the back of his wagon. He must have made ten trips to get all those pieces home.

Donny was always doing some home improvement project or tinkering around in the yard. As he drove home from the firehouse, he began to go over in his head some of the tasks for the day ahead. He had to stain some molding for the dining room. Maybe he'd get everything ready and take the project with him to the firehouse, which had a makeshift carpentry shop in the basement. Either way, he was going to get to hang out with his best buddy, Nicky. When Donny got home, around eight A.M., Linda was fixing the three-year-old his breakfast.

Upstairs, the eldest three sons were getting dressed for school. Don junior was a funny, outgoing boy with a fresh rash of pimples and a mop of wavy brown hair. He had just started his freshman year at nearby Bishop Timon High School. Donny had looked forward to the day when one of his boys would attend Timon. Run by Franciscan priests, Timon may not have been as academically rigorous as some of the other private Catholic high schools in Buffalo, but there was discipline and tradition. And tuition. Donny had spent the summer fixing roofs and putting up aluminum siding to earn extra money to help cover the four-thousand-dollar-per-year nut, all while spearheading major renovations at his mom and dad's home on Melrose Street, not to mention working full-time as a firefighter.

Time was catching up to Donny. He was thirty-four and looked every one of those years. He never stopped.

On a mere moment's notice Donny would happily fill in as a substitute gym teacher at St. Agatha's or help run bingo night. Earlier that summer, Donny filled in as a late replacement godfather for his brother-in-law Patrick's first-born son, Matthew. Patrick, who was Linda's younger brother, wanted Donny to be one of the godparents in the first place, but as it turned out his wife, Jen, chose her cousin John for the role. For whatever reason, Cousin John bailed out at the last minute. Donny was there, he had a tie on, and most of all, St. Agatha's pastor Robert Yetter knew full well he regularly attended ten o'clock Mass every Sunday.

Later that same summer, a few weeks before the start of the school year, Donny found himself excited to be a part of the Timon community again. He wandered over to his old high school to find out whether he might volunteer in some way. The priests took him up on the offer, putting him right to work that afternoon in the school's gymnasium, which was in need of a fresh coat of paint. Rummaging through a cluttered storage area in search of a drop cloth, Donny had come across the old "peg board," an archaic wooden climbing apparatus that was once affixed to one of the gym's walls. Donny, lean but in possession of freakish upper-body strength, had mastered it as a student. Discarded, dusty, the outdated piece of equipment was nonetheless in fairly decent condition. Donny cleaned it off and, with a carpenter's steady touch, lovingly returned the old peg board to serve a new generation of strong and able South Buffalo boys.

In a few years Donny and Linda would have three boys enrolled at Timon at the same time. Don junior was consistently earning top grades. Tommy, an eighth grader at St. Agatha's, excelled in every sport he played—soccer, baseball, track, basketball, football. Patrick, a chubby eleven-year-old, in his own way was a family fulcrum. He quietly did what he was told and looked after his little brother Nicky.

Donny wouldn't pick favorites when it came to his own children. However, the baby, Nicky, was indisputably his new best buddy. With Nick being so much younger, and Donny's four-days-on, four-days-off schedule, the two grew about as close as an adult man and a toddler could. Donny loved to pal around with "little Nicky." The boy went everywhere with him. Everyone in the neighborhood knew Nick; he was like a little adult, shadowing Donny while Donny worked in the yard, wearing a plastic yellow work helmet and pedaling about in a miniature toy forklift truck.

Donny wasn't due back at the firehouse until evening. With the whole gorgeous Indian summer day in front of him, he set about making a plan.

"Hey, Lin, what do you say me, you, and Nicky take a drive over to Tifft Farm," Donny suggested. "Get some fresh air."

By now it was around eleven A.M., and the sunshine was pouring in through the kitchen windows.

"Sounds good," Linda said. "It's way too nice to be inside."

Donny, a true outdoorsman who during the season sometimes woke up at four A.M. to go bow hunting in the Southern Tier at sunrise, savored any opportunity to connect with nature. He cherished these walks around Tifft Nature Preserve with Linda and the kids. There was really not much there—brownish ponds, a hilly clearing, some tree-lined trails. Sometimes they'd spy a sprinting deer or a broad-winged hawk, but just to be walking around outside, together, drinking in the breeze and the sunshine—that was all they needed.

Once an old dairy farm, the 260-acre Tifft site comprised mainly of cattail marshes, was for much of the 1950s and 1960s a municipal dumping ground. Redeveloped as a landfill site, Tifft Farm in the mid-1970s was designated as a wildlife sanctuary, improbable as that might have seemed considering it was surrounded by factories, mills, railroad yards, and junkyards. But the refuge was built, and the wildlife came, including more than two hundred species of migratory birds—horned larks, woodcocks, warblers, depending on the time of year.

Linda loaded Nicky into the Caprice, an American classic with a roof rack and fake wood panels, the fourth in a series of semireliable Herbert family station wagons. Donny, a nonbeliever in the concept of monthly car payments, had purchased a used wagon for roughly eight hundred dollars cash each of the past few years around tax refund time. Some of them lasted longer than others. One wagon ended up totaled on the front lawn of St. Agatha's only minutes after its purchase, while another caught fire in a Kmart parking lot.

The Caprice was one of the better wagons, and spacious—though the entire back was filled with Donny's tools. They drove down Durant Street, which in just a few short years had sprouted a handful of simple homes.

From Durant Street, the Herberts took a right turn onto Spaulding, passing the corner house in which Linda and her ten brothers and sisters grew up, then a left on Hopkins, then over the Tifft Street Bridge spanning the great rail yards. The entrance to the nature preserve was down on Fuhrmann Boulevard near the base of the Skyway, an elevated stretch of wind-battered thruway that hugged the edge of steel gray Lake Erie. They parked in an empty lot and began their stroll down a narrow trail marked by a worn-out Parks Department plaque. The path led to the top of a grassy, sloping hill, upon which sat a paint-chipped park bench. Donny, in a pair of gray work pants and a navy blue BFD T-shirt, sat down with Nicky on his lap. He leaned his head back and closed his eyes— did that sun ever feel good.

"Smile," Linda said, clicking a quick photo of the two best pals sharing the bench and the puffy-clouded blue sky. Donny was squinting, his powerful forearm snuggling Nicky tight. In the distance, the abandoned Cargill grain elevators appeared to loom right over the lake.

"I think I might just sit here all day," Donny announced, running his fingers through Nicky's white-blond hair, grinning at his wife. They had had their ups and downs over the years. No marriage was perfect. But at the core, their love was as strong as ever.

The Herberts had the breezy habitat all to themselves. A civil servant who made around thirty-five thousand dollars a year, who owned a house built on an abandoned street with a government grant, who drove around in a secondhand car, and whose most valuable personal possessions consisted of a hodgepodge set of old tools, a bow, some arrows, a few fishing rods, and a tackle box, Donny would never be considered a wealthy man. And yet he had just about everything he could ever want. If Donny needed anything, it was probably just to slow down.

Five

NORMALLY, THE HOLIDAYS were a happy time, but for some reason during that bitingly cold December of 1995, the weight of the world was pressing down hard on Donny Herbert. And sometimes even the sturdiest shoulders can only take so much.

He and Linda had been quarreling. The kids seemed to be constantly stirring up trouble around the house, which in itself seemed to linger in a perpetual state of renovation and repair. If someone called Donny on the phone, it was usually because they needed something. Money was always tight.

Meanwhile, Rescue 1 and Engine 3 had just come off a nasty run of treacherous fires. Donny didn't look himself. A stressful, worrisome countenance replaced his normally upbeat, seize-the-moment glimmer. One of Donny's best friends in the department, Gary O'Neill, confronted him during the middle of a live fire and demanded to know what was the matter. "I don't know," Donny had said, dropping to the floor Indian-style, smoke wafting all around him. "I'm tired."

For all his energy and zeal, being wherever he was needed, Donny could no longer keep up the way he once did. Sure, he still enjoyed firefighting, but the Rescue 1 crew, sometimes rushing from one tragic occurrence to the next nonstop, was sorely overworked. The Christmas season full of delightful Herbert family traditions, such as cutting down their tree—always out on some farm in the middle of nowhere and always involving some form of misadventure—somehow had been replaced by shopping and scheduling, headaches and hurry, with Donny and Linda and the four kids shuffling from one pageant, performance, party, or practice to the next. There was constantly a pile of unmet expectations. Donny's mother needed siding put up, his brother needed jumper cables, Linda had errands for him. Then Linda would complain he was never there to do things for her. When, Donny wondered, did it end?

ON CHRISTMAS EVE Donny and Linda took the boys to St. Agatha's for seven P.M. Mass. Nicky and Patty were playing shepherds in the nativity pageant, so before they left Linda had taken lots of photos of the costumed children. After church, the family set out on a holiday ramble, first over to Donny's parents on Melrose Street for some eggnog and to exchange a few gifts. Then it was off to visit

Uncle Simon and his family in Orchard Park, and then back to South Buffalo for traditional Christmas Eve mayhem at Linda's parents' house on Spaulding.

There, in the kitchen, Donny seemed fatigued, unsettled, almost like a man at the end of his rope. Linda's sister Teresa had just stopped by. It was late, and she'd wanted to give Donny a present. Normally, Teresa and Donny did not exchange gifts; he had not gotten anything for her. But this was special. Teresa had picked it up on an impulse earlier that day while searching for a last-minute gift for a coworker at Woolworth's. It was a VHS copy of Frank Capra's *It's a Wonderful Life*.

"My favorite," Donny exclaimed.

"I saw it today while I was in line and I thought, 'Oh, I have got to get this for Donny,'" Teresa said.

"Thanks," Donny whispered, kissing Teresa on the cheek, which she found a bit melodramatic.

Donny looked genuinely touched, almost misty eyed, an odd reaction to a ten-dollar videocassette tape.

Strange, Teresa thought. What was on Donny's mind?

ONE DAY AFTER CHRISTMAS, which had fallen on a Monday, Donny and Linda were planning for Nicky's fourth birthday party; nothing too extraordinary, a few relatives over at their house for cake. The gathering would have been held right on Nicky's actual birthday, December 27, except that John Breier and his wife, Irene, were having their annual holiday party that same night. Despite the busy rush of the holidays, Donny and Linda always looked forward to and made time for the Breier affair. In fact, on the Wednesday night of the party, they opted to leave fourteen-year-old Don junior in charge of his three little brothers for the very first time—a big deal for everyone involved. "You're the man of the house tonight," Donny told his son. The words could not have had more importance. Don junior promised he would be fine. He was, after all, a freshman at Timon. Later, Linda would recall having one of the most enjoyable nights out in a long time, sharing a few drinks and laughs with Donny, chatting with the other firemen and their wives, just plain socializing without any cares for a change. She owed much of her relaxing evening to the trust she had put in Don junior that night, and he lived up to the task.

The plan then was to celebrate Nicky's birthday on Friday night, December 29. Time was tight. The day before, Thursday, Donny's sister Jeanne had organized a once-in-a-decade Herbert family photograph, with their father and mother and grandmother and all of the children and grandchildren. As a result, Donny knew he would be late for the five P.M. start of his fifteen-hour overnight shift, and so he had arranged for someone to stay a little longer to cover for him, until five-thirty. The staging of the portrait, along the grand staircase of a Delaware Avenue mansion-studio, took a lot longer than anyone had expected, and afterward each family was having separate family photos taken. It was getting close to six P.M. As he waited for his family's turn, Donny grew edgy. He had to leave. Linda knew he was stressed.

"Just go," she said. "We have plenty of photos. Go on."

She was slightly irked, but at the same time she more than understood his having to relieve another fireman. Upon his green light, Donny bolted down the plush stairs. Linda called out after him.

"Hey, don't forget we're doing Nicky's birthday tomorrow night!"

"I haven't forgotten," Donny called back. "It's going to be great."

About twenty minutes later, Linda and the four boys had a family portrait taken without him.

THE PHONE RANG on Durant Street at around eleven-thirty P.M. on December 28. It was Donny.

He'd called Linda from the quiet of the empty fire-house kitchen. "I can't sleep," he told her. "Talk to me."

"What's wrong?"

"I don't know."

"What do you mean?"

Donny paused. Linda could tell he was choking back tears. "I just . . . feel like no matter what I do it's never enough."

"Aw, Don—"

"No, I'm telling you, I can't keep going like this. I can't be there for everybody all the time. Something has to give."

"Don, listen to me," Linda said. "I know what you're going through. I've had anxiety attacks, remember? I know what they're like. I think you're having one right now. You just need to take a deep breath. Everything's going to be okay."

Donny's emotions were catching up with him. He loved her and those kids so much it hurt.

"But you're going to have to make some changes. You've got to slow down. You can't do everything. I need you here. The kids need you."

"You're right." Donny sighed. "I am going to make some changes. I have to slow down."

"You just need to learn how to say no."

Donny and Linda talked for another ten minutes, discussing what final things needed to be taken care of for Nicky's party the next night; one of them needed to pick up a few snacks and some pop. Donny mentioned that he had tickets for a Bills-Dolphins wild card playoff game Saturday, and Linda encouraged him to go with his friends. Even with the Bills winning the AFC championship seemingly every year, Donny hadn't been to a game at Rich Stadium since Joe Ferguson was quarterback.

"I'll be home in the morning," Donny said, feeling better but still nagged by something he couldn't quite put his finger on. It was close to midnight.

"Are you going be okay?" Linda asked.

"I think so," Donny said. "Lin, something *just doesn't seem right.*"

"Well, you call me if you want to talk—no matter how late, okay, hon?"

"Okay, Lin. Thanks."

"Good night; love you."

"Love you, too."

Donny hung up the phone and, unable to sleep, sat down in the firehouse kitchen to watch some television with Gary O'Neill, who couldn't sleep either.

On Durant Street, Linda returned to her empty bed and placed the cordless phone on the pillow next to her in case Donny called back. But he did not.

THE SEQUENCE OF three long tones signaling a structure fire came in over the radio speakers at 6:13 A.M. on Friday, December 29. They were followed by the crackle of the dispatcher's phantom monotone: "An alarm of fire, Twenty-one Inter Park between Fillmore and Humboldt . . ."

Over Donny's head in the bunk room, a seventy-five-decibel bell began ringing. He woke from a dead sleep and leapt right up, the first man down the stairs, as usual. He made it onto the apparatus floor and into his gear—turnout coat, bunker pants, boots, gloves—a full minute before his lieutenant on the rescue truck, Paddy Coghlan, older and slower moving, had even gotten out of bed. Following right behind Donny were two other members of Rescue 1, Jerry Nostrant, a twenty-seven-year-old St. Ambrose kid whom Donny had taken under his wing, and a nine-year-veteran, Jim Wellenzohn.

Already downstairs, manning the four A.M. to eight A.M. watch, was Gary O'Neill, first to hear the alarm come in. Outside, the world had been blanketed by a few inches of snow and it was still coming down lightly. The streets were already covered by the remnants of a major storm two weeks earlier that brought three feet of snow. Factoring in wind chill, the temperature hovered at around five degrees. One alarm had sounded, so for the moment just the five-man Rescue 1 would head out. Soon enough, though, Gary and the rest of Engine 3 would be called over.

"Where we going?" Donny asked his comrade as he pulled on his boots.

"Twenty-one Inter Park," Gary replied.

An electrical fire had broken out in the second-floor ceiling of a large two-and-a-half-story wood-frame apartment house located in the bowels of Buffalo's inner city. From the radio traffic it sounded to Gary like a working fire.

Outside it was still pitch-dark. As firefighter Jerry Johnson warmed up the Rescue 1 truck, Donny stood by the doorway, cigarette hanging out of his mouth, the thick Kevlar sleeves of his turnout coat rolled up. Seeing the men geared up and almost ready to head out to the fire, Gary pushed the Open button over the watch desk. The front doors of the firehouse came up.

"See you," Gary called out to Donny as Johnson moved the Rescue rig out. Lieutenant Coghlan was in the passenger seat next to him. Jim Wellenzohn was in the jump seat on the driver's side of the rig. Donny hung off the pole on the back, in the box, cigarette in his free hand. As the first blare of the siren sliced through the frigid, predawn air, Donny looked back at Gary and waved him a sullen good-bye.

IT TOOK SIX MINUTES for Rescue 1 to arrive; a left on Broadway, two blocks up to Jefferson, a right on Jefferson, over to Route 33, two exits toward downtown to East Ferry near Fillmore Avenue. The house on Inter Park was near the corner of Humboldt, one block north of East Ferry. Quickly on the scene were three engine companies, 33, 21, and 18, as well as two ladder companies, 6 and 11.

"Look at all that smoke," muttered Jerry Nostrant, who was standing in the box next to Donny in the back of the Rescue truck, which had pulled up a half block away, its path to the fire blocked by snow banks and Engine 18's rig. The entire street seemed engulfed in a heavy black cloud. Neither Jerry nor Donny could even tell which house was on fire until they were right in front of it. The fire, meanwhile, had spread to the attic, a cluttered storage space.

Engine 21, led by Captain Jimmy Seemueller, was setting up an exposure line—one hose dedicated to surrounding property exposed to the fire—in an alley between the
burning house and the one next door. Donny put on his
face piece. Ax in hand, a thirty-minute tank of oxygen
strapped to his back, he soldiered up the front porch stairs.

A skilled nozzle man, Dan Benning of Engine 33, along
with his lieutenant, Mike "Mac" McCarthy, were on the
second floor, working an attack line. Their mission: get
to the attic and confront the blaze head-on. At any fire
scene, the firefighters of Rescue 1, this morning being led
by Lieutenant Coghlan, could be utilized at the division
chief's disposal, whether that meant helping to ventilate,
manning a ladder pipe, or performing search and rescue.
Acting division chief that morning was Joe Brocato;
Captain Tony Page of Engine 31, the acting battalion chief,
was second in command, although before any formal plan
for rescue's deployment could be articulated by either
Brocato, Page, or Coghlan, Donny, rarely one to have to be
told what to do at a fire, rushed up to the second floor to
assist in a search for possible victims.

The stairway leading to the second floor and the attic
was located in the rear of the house, near the kitchen.
Donny proceeded up to assist the hose men, Benning and
McCarthy. They'd dragged their line to just below the attic
floor landing, battling the heat and smoke. But inch by
inch they had advanced. Donny was prepared to crawl

ahead and knock out the windows to air out some of the blinding smoke. But when Engine 33 turned on the hose, every ounce of water turned into boiling steam that left Donny, McCarthy, and Benning as well as a crew from Ladder 11 scrambling back down the stairs. Every time they tried to push up to the attic, the heat and the steam became too intense. "Those guys are taking a beating," said Captain Page, who was outside ordering two firefighters to the roof. "I need that thing open!"

Meanwhile, Brocato kept tight control of the stairs and the hallway leading to it, ordering some firemen back down to the second floor. "I want those stairs clear!" he insisted.

Brocato ordered two firefighters to man hose lines from the top of the attic stairs. McCarthy and Benning, out of air, had gone back down to replenish their tanks. Rescue 1's Jerry Nostrant and a firefighter from Engine 18, Jerry Nappo, took over their lines. Both firefighters were positioned at the top of the attic stairs, aiming their hoses toward a flimsy drop ceiling flames had breached. A burning hole exposed a two-foot section between the ceiling and the rafters, a gap known as a cockloft.

Donny, who'd held his position on the landing but was now almost out of air, rushed back down the stairs, his tank alarm ringing.

"Man, is it hot up there!" he exclaimed as he passed Nostrant.

The heat in the attic was insufferable.

Nostrant and Nappo were now out of air; Benning and McCarthy, tanks refilled, returned and resumed hose duty. Benning was feeding McCarthy the line around a sharp bend in the stairwell. Two firemen from Ladder 11, Billy Sanford and Mike Sequin, had just gone up to the roof on the ventilation detail. Donny, meanwhile, had refilled his tank and was heading back up to the attic.

Word had spread that all occupants were believed to have gotten out and were accounted for, but the fire was still raging in the attic, a half-story covered by a flat, mansard-style roof. As such it was laden down, not only by a few feet of ice and snow, but by several layers of asphalt and wooden shingles as well. Weakened, charred two-by-four beams across opposite walls shuddered.

The fire was nearly contained, but not without a solid drag-out bout. Passing Benning, who was manning the hose on the stairs, Donny told him, "I got the windows." Lieutenant McCarthy, Donny, and Chief Brocato had managed to enter the attic. All other fireman were told to stay downstairs. Donny and McCarthy set out across opposite sides of the floor toward the front of the house, looking for hot spots in the walls and inching closer to the front attic windows. Heavy smoke obscured the gross clutter of soot- and water-soaked cardboard boxes. Up on the roof, the two firefighters from Ladder 11, Sanford and Sequin, had managed to get to the center.

Brocato walked toward the middle of the attic to survey what was happening. Just then, at precisely 6:54 A.M., Lieutenant McCarthy noticed one of the two-by-four rafters above the ravaged drop ceiling appear to buckle. Not one second later, the roof caved in, taking Sanford and Sequin with it.

From one end of the ridge line across to the other, the beams split and the ceiling imploded, folding in on itself in a V shape with a sickening whoosh as snow, ice, rafters, drywall, soot, and roofing material came crashing down.

Through the smoky haze, Brocato felt a crash of beams on either side of him. Looking around he saw Sanford and Sequin, both of whom were just as surprised to see him considering what an unholy mess had just poured down upon the chief.

"Chief, you okay?" Sanford asked.

"Yeah. Where did you guys come from?"

"Chief, we were on the roof."

Confused, Brocato looked around—indeed, he had been standing right in the middle of the implosion and the entire roof above his head had come down on both sides of him like a scene from an old Buster Keaton film. Sanford and Sequin had tumbled headlong into the fold-in wreckage pile, Sequin landing on top of Sanford. From where he was standing at the top of the stairs leading into the attic, Dan Benning had been smacked in the head by the force of the collapsing beams. Benning was swatted down to the second-floor landing like a pinball.

"Come on, we got guys trapped!" Brocato yelled, motioning for Sanford and Sequin to start digging. Sanford took one swing toward the front of the attic where he heard yelling. "That's my foot!" He had struck McCarthy's boot, which was sticking out of the rubble.

Clawing furiously with their bare hands, Sanford and Sequin proceeded to pull Mac out of the tangled heap of beams and debris. He'd been hit in the head and nicked by Sanford's ax, but he seemed okay and remained conscious.

"Did you guys see Donny Herbert?" McCarthy asked.

None of them had. Two minutes had gone by since the collapse.

"Is Donny Herbert out there?" Brocato screamed. "Has anyone seen Donny Herbert?" a line of firemen repeated in a chain of shouts, one after the other, a dreadful roll call to which there was no reply. Within seconds the interdepartment radio channels alerted firemen around the city that one of their own was in trouble. "Companies in the attic," called out Captain Tony Page over the radio. "The roof just fell in."

Back at headquarters, Deputy Commissioner Jack Sniderhan got a phone call from the dispatcher, who told him, "We got a man trapped in a working fire."

"Man trapped!" Page shouted again.

Not far away at his home in an area known as Lovejoy, a still sleepy John Breier had just put in his hearing aids when the grim chatter—"*Somebody's trapped in the attic*"—came over the scanner that the retired Rescue 1 driver kept in his living room. His heart sank. "It's Herby," he told his wife, Irene, who was putting on a pot of coffee. "I just know it's Herby."

"HE WAS RIGHT OVER THERE," McCarthy gasped, pointing to the opposite pile of debris some fifteen feet across the attic. About three minutes had elapsed since the roof caved in. By this time, the smoke had cleared in the open air, although the debris pile, which had created a double lean-to effect with a single trench down the middle, still crackled and smoldered.

Frantically, Sequin and Sanford made their way toward the front of the attic, hacking at the beams with their axes, unsure of whether the floor might give next. Outside, Page ordered ladders to the front of the house. At this point no one knew the full extent of structural damage, nor was it an immediate concern: All any of them cared about was finding Donny. The only way into this mess for the firemen outside was up ladders to the attic window; the back stairway had been demolished in the collapse.

Brocato, Sanford, and Sequin's search for Donny grew more frenzied. The fire by now was under control, but some lingering smoke and blowing soot made it difficult to see. As they surveyed the rubble, a woozy Mac McCarthy did his best to point out the spot where Donny should have been. Sanford cut a gaping hole in the side of the fallen roof and peered in. He could see an air tank.

Finally, six full minutes after the roof had caved in, they saw Donny, almost exactly where McCarthy had estimated he would be. He was sitting up, unconscious, pinned under a fallen beam, his head bent forward at a ninety-degree angle.

Six

RACING TIME AS they stared down another collapse, a half dozen or so courageous Buffalo firemen got up on a porch roof below the attic window. Having hacked their way through to Donny, Sanford and Sequin had had to literally pick the roof up off him. They got down low, dug in their shoulders, and somehow propped it up. Once they had freed Donny, firefighter Joe Victor, who had managed to climb up through the front attic window, quickly gave Donny four mouth-to-mouth breaths and hurled him through the attic window. Engine 18's Tom Jackson, among the biggest men on the whole department at six foot three and 260 pounds, single-handedly carried Donny down the ladder to the front yard. Within seconds, a thirteen-year veteran, Walter Jones, one of Donny's instructors at the training academy, began to administer oxygen and perform CPR. But Donny wasn't breathing. An ambulance was approaching down the street, which was blocked by department rigs and unplowed snow, so a group of a half dozen firefighters loaded Donny onto a stretcher and hurriedly sloshed him down the street like a pack of sled dogs. Greg Halbina, a Rescue 1 relief man who'd just come on the scene with the crew from Engine 3, jumped into the ambulance and continued to perform CPR. Donny was gray, but he had a pulse.

The ambulance took off for Erie County Medical Center. McCarthy and Benning were also rushed to the hospital, but only Donny was in critical condition.

With a police escort leading the way, a shrill procession of ambulances and fire department vehicles, including one carrying Fire Commissioner Cornelius Keane, raced south along the eastern border of the city, as the sun started to creep across the horizon.

Father Joe, emergency services chaplain, had also rushed to ECMC. Monsignor Clody, the fire chaplain, had stayed on at the chaotic Inter Park scene. Jack Sniderhan, deputy fire commissioner, drove Father Joe to the hospital. When they arrived, there were firemen everywhere, all concerned about Donny.

"Oh, my God," Father Joe Bayne cried out in the crowded ECMC hallway. "We've got to get Linda!"

The young priest was worried sick. He had grown close to Donny and his family over the past few years. Bad memories of his own father being killed in a fire fused with his worst fears. *Oh God, not again.* Father Joe prepared for the worst, praying for anything but.

It had dawned on him that in all the confusion no one

had yet thought to notify Donny's family. Video footage of the fire would be on the local morning news programs. "Come on, Jack," Father Joe told the deputy commissioner. "We've got to go get Linda," the young priest said as he reached for an Erie County–issue mobile phone.

Inside the mazelike ECMC emergency room area, the Buffalo Fire Department had taken over. A dozen or more firemen charged right into the emergency room with Donny and a dozen more were streaming into the waiting room, adjacent examination rooms and hallways, all of them still reeking of the Inter Park fire. Other firemen just getting off work around the city also arrived. Soon there were more than a hundred of BFD's bravest on hand.

As the deputy commissioner drove quietly into South Buffalo, Father Joe dialed the Herbert home. Linda had taken her cordless phone to bed with her. She answered on the second ring. It was around seven-fifteen A.M.

"Linda, it's Father Joe. There's been an accident—Donny's been injured."

"How bad is he?"

Father Joe paused, delivering the truth couched in hope.

"He does have a pulse and the doctors are working on him right now. We're on our way over to get you. Do you have someone to watch the boys? Linda, if anyone can get through something like this, it's Donny. . . ."

Linda felt sick as her heart began to race. She put on

her robe and came out of the bedroom. The kids were all home on Christmas vacation, but only young Don was up, yawning in the hallway outside his bedroom door, already frightened by the troubling fragment of his mother's end of the unsettling wake-up call.

"What's going on?"

"Your dad's been hurt in a fire," Linda said. "Father Joe is on his way over to take me to ECMC. I think it's bad."

Her eldest son's stomach tightened in anguish. Just a few days ago, his dad had made him the man of the house. Not this. This couldn't be happening.

"Oh no . . ."

Father Joe and Deputy Commissioner Sniderhan were in the Herberts' driveway within minutes. Linda, nervous, determined at least to try to stay calm, came out to meet them. Right then, Linda's father drove by on his way to work as the head custodian at Southside High School. He took one look at the fire department vehicle and the expression on his daughter's face, pulled over his car, and backed up to the house.

"It's Don," Linda said.

She didn't have to say anything else. Her father returned home to 77 Spaulding a few hundred yards away to tell Linda's mother, who then called Linda's older sister Teresa, who began to spread the word to the other siblings.

The deputy commissioner's Crown Victoria sped past

other fire trucks on the way to ECMC, each one filled with men anxious to find out what had happened to Donny and to the other injured firefighters. Inside the vehicle, Linda was trapped in her worst nightmare. The blare of sirens created its own uneasy silence. All Linda kept thinking to herself over and over was, *Please, God, let him be okay.*

With Father Joe by her side, Linda rushed through the entrance to the emergency room. Everywhere she looked she saw firefighters still in uniform. The smell of smoke was overpowering.

Linda was led into a small room, where Donny, ashen and filthy, was hooked up to a ventilator, a breathing tube taped in the corner of his mouth. EEG and EKG devices monitored brain and heart activity. Wires and lines crisscrossed haphazardly with suction tubes and multiple IVs. The sporadic beeping of the equipment and ominous *swoosh* of the bulky breathing machine grated on Linda's nerves. Donny was out of it. Physically he didn't look too bad—he had just some facial burns. But Linda knew it was bad.

Dr. Alan Posner, a lanky trauma specialist in his late thirties who had taken charge of the scene, told Linda right away that he was worried about oxygen loss and potential brain damage. The EEG recordings of the electrical signals coming from Donny's brain showed abnormally slow activity. In addition to a tremendous blow to the head, Donny had suffocated and doctors believed his heart had momentarily stopped. His face piece and air tank had become dislodged in the crush of smoldering debris. Even if the oxygen had been flowing normally, his head and neck were hyperextended, pinned forward at an awful angle by a fallen beam, resulting, doctors theorized, in slow asphyxiation. After only one minute without oxygen, brain tissue begins to die. After three minutes, entire sections of the brain can be wiped clean. Six minutes and there is catastrophic damage. And Donny appeared to have been trapped without air for at least six minutes. Those who survive such prolonged deprivation almost always emerge in a permanent vegetative condition. As he lay unconscious, Donny's pulse was weak, and his vital signs were volatile. No one was quite sure whether he was going to make it. The next few hours would tell.

"Hang on, Donny," Linda said. She was shaking, crying. "I love you. I need you. We need you."

Linda dropped her head in her hands and prayed to herself. *Please, Lord. I can't raise these kids alone.*

Seven

BETWEEN THE HUNDREDS of concerned firemen, dozens of grief-stricken family members on both sides, and persistent local television news people, the ECMC intensive care unit became something of a three-ring circus in the twenty-four hours following Donny's injury. Raw nervous energy gave way to helpful deeds. Jimmy Seemueller shuttled to and from the waiting room offering food and coffee, back and forth, all day. Linda was allowed to see her husband for only twenty minutes at a time, once every four hours. She'd been unaware that all three local television stations were running the dramatic film of Donny being hoisted out of the front attic window of the roofless Inter Park home. Back on Durant Street, the Herbert boys, all on Christmas vacation, watched the footage over and over, in numbed disbelief. *Why us?* Linda's mother and sisters stayed with them, trying to keep their hopes up. "Your dad is getting all the medical care he needs right now," Debbie told them. All of the boys were taking it hard, except for Nicky, too young to understand what was happening.

That evening, Debbie, Peggy, Jean, and Teresa picked up a birthday cake and rounded up the despondent brothers to give Nicky a full-on four-candle salute, as cheerfully as they could, in part to reclaim some shred of goodness, but above all to stay busy.

Back at the ICU burn unit, Donny was clinging to life. Heading up his medical team was Dr. Posner, visibly annoyed by the overflowing crowd in the waiting room and hallways. The tragedy drew an incredible outpouring of concern from friends and citywide condolences. Bishop Henry Mansell, Mayor Tony Masiello, Fire Commissioner Keane—all came by. But few of them knew quite what to say to Linda, who was distraught to the point of speechlessness. Most visitors whispered a quick offering of support or let her be. Linda asked them to pray.

The ICU wing was massive, comprising several large glass-enclosed rooms, with a bustling nurses' station in the center. Donny lay motionless in the burn-unit room, quiet but for the creepy whir of the ventilator breathing on his behalf.

As the hours wore on, Linda began to worry more about the boys. They loved their dad so much. How could they ever bear to lose him?

Please, God, stay with him. Please bring him back to us.

THAT SPRING, the actor Christopher Reeve had had a riding accident that left him paralyzed. Shocked to see news footage of Superman in a quadriplegic state, Donny specifically told Linda that if anything like that ever happened to him, to please do whatever she could to make sure he did not live like that. Linda was reminded of this as Dr. Posner explained that if Donny did survive, he might have permanent brain damage. She wondered fleetingly in the dark hours that next long Saturday if maybe it was better that Donny died. But in the quiet of the waiting room area early Sunday morning, she knew in her heart that every day he survived in itself was another giant accomplishment, and that she would take any Donny she could get. She would care for him, just as he had taken such good care of her and the boys.

"I need him here," she sobbed to her best friend, Luanne, who was by her side the entire time. "I don't care how bad. In any form, some form, whatever. I need him *here.*"

THE NEXT FEW DAYS seemed to run together as one endless loop of torment and tears. Linda stayed at the hospital most of the time, but went home regularly to check on the boys. A full battalion of Buffalo firemen was at her call as a chauffeur and concierge service. All the while, the late December weather continued to howl nastily. Snow, more snow, and brutally cold temperatures. Linda managed to attend ten o'clock Mass on Sunday with the boys. Donny would have been there. His absence pummeled Linda as she sat looking around the pews. It was December 31, the first Sunday after Christmas, the Feast of the Holy Family. One of the readings that day included an Old Testament passage (Sirach 3:6-12) that shook her to the core.

> *He who reveres his father will live a long life; he obeys the Lord who brings comfort to his mother . . . My son, take care of your father . . . Even if his mind fail, be considerate with him. For kindness to a father will not be forgotten.*

Linda, with Don junior offering his shoulder, wept. She vowed to do everything she could for Donny. Just as the Bible advised.

THAT SUNDAY NIGHT, New Year's Eve, unbeknownst to Linda, all of her siblings—Jack, Sharon, Peggy, Teresa, Debbie, Mary, Jean, Patrick, Michael, and David—held an emotional family meeting at the Buffalo Irish Center, a gin mill/town hall down the street from St. Agatha's on Abbott Road. Teresa made sure everyone was notified. It was a somber yet recuperative affair, a badly needed outlet to talk things over, but mostly to plan for the worst. Donny was clinging to life, and no one thought, realistically, that he would make it. Soon, some major decisions and sacrifices would have to be made. Everyone would need to pitch in, with money and time.

The second youngest of the clan, Michael, a soft-spoken twenty-three-year-old, came trudging in last. Shaking the snow off his boots, he mentioned to his sister Teresa that he had come from shoveling snow from the front walkway of their grandmother Yvonne's apartment. No one had asked him to, but he felt it had to be done. The old woman lived alone in a small complex for seniors a few blocks away. Michael, always the most sensitive one, had taken Donny's accident extremely hard.

"That was nice of you," Teresa said.

Michael stared down at the floor and muttered a soft reply. "It's what Donny would have done."

Eight

NICKY WAS AGITATED. He wanted his daddy. Soon, his mom told him, soon she would take him to the place where Daddy was. It had been days and days, which to Nicky seemed like forever. He would not stop his campaign. "When am I going to see Daddy?"

Linda realized he was starting to figure things out, and she could tell this by his uncharacteristic behavior. He was fidgety, disobedient. Though she'd done her best to shield the little guy, and as painful as it was to confront, Linda knew eventually she owed Nicky an explanation. At some point she was also going to have to start toting him along with her to ECMC. She had no choice. On the Wednesday after Donny's accident, she decided to take Nicky to see his dad.

For hours they sat in the waiting room, in metal chairs. Nicky was fascinated by the row of large cabinets that lined the room, many of them stuffed with pillows and blankets. But he was turning downright unruly. "I want to see Daddy!" he screamed, not crying but clearly one frustrated four-year-old. There were other families around them in varying states of shock and grief, having to deal with their own tragedies: a terrible car accident, a fight turned ugly, a sudden unexplained illness. Finally, the nurse came and took Linda and Nicky into the ICU.

Linda held her youngest boy up to the glass wall encasing his father's room. Nick pressed his face right up to it so hard his nose hurt. Inside the narrow room, Donny, despite the tubes crammed in his mouth connecting him to the ventilator, looked himself and seemed to be resting comfortably.

"Your dad's just sleeping right now," Linda conned. "Can you see him?"

The boy nodded yes, he could. He could see Daddy asleep.

Nick was fine after that. Linda was able to keep him by her side without too much trouble. He adapted surprisingly well to his new routine: hanging around the waiting room until the nurse came, donning surgical masks and gowns for the brief trips to his father's bedside, hastily discarding the gowns in the big plastic bag by the doorway before going back to the waiting room. Nick mastered the hallways, where they led, and in time discovered the humongous cafeteria filled with endless rows of tables to crawl under, although his favorite pastime was exploring the hospital's many cabinets, sliding nooks, and storage rooms. These private scavenger hunts more often than not yielded a trove of funny toy balloons better known as surgical gloves.

Donny was still unconscious, unable to breathe on his own. Doctors diagnosed him as having suffered one of the most unsparing types of head trauma known, in medical terms a *severe anoxic brain injury,* that is, an injury caused by oxygen deprivation. Simultaneously and just as devastating, Donny had suffered a heavy blow to the head by the roof timbers—his firefighter's helmet had the dent to prove it. Because of the extremely sensitive nature of human gray matter, even minor head trauma could cause irreparable damage.

His *entire* brain had been traumatized, seemingly wiped away like the motherboard of a crashed computer.

As January wore on his vital signs stabilized, and at times he seemed to yawn or even smile. He moved his arms, and while he was impossible to understand because of the breathing tubes, he appeared a few times to be trying to speak. Donny had technically emerged from a comatose state because he appeared to have distinct sleeping and waking states, and he was opening and closing his eyes. But for the most part he was unresponsive to the world around him. Dr. Posner had done a CT scan, which indicated some degree of damage to most if not all parts of Donny's brain. His injury could not have been worse—severe head trauma *and* oxygen deprivation. The occipital lobe, located at the back of the brain and believed to control vision was fried. The temporal lobe, from which, among other things, speech activity originates, was equally scorched of living brain tissue. Yet somehow Donny's brain, like an out-of-gas car running on fumes, churned out enough signal transmissions from its stem to keep his involuntary muscles in play, to keep his heart pumping, his vital organs working, even as he displayed scant brain-wave activity.

But every day Donny made it through was in itself a big deal, a step closer to living, to some kind of recovery. *But with what damage?* Linda was praying the rosary and asking that everyone, please, pray. Meanwhile, cards and letters were streaming in from total strangers around the city. Father Joe Moreno, the police chaplain, came by almost every day with goodies from Gino's bakery, so often that Linda and the kids began calling him "Father Cannoli."

The firefighters, not just the guys in Donny's house but from all over the department, pitched in however they could. They sat with the family, volunteered to run errands, and provided rides. They cooked buckets of food, donated mobile phones and pagers for all the kids, even shoveled snow from the Herberts' driveway. They did everything they could. And they were praying, too.

The never-ending, indeed continually expanding, throng of visitors in and around the ECMC waiting room area—television reporters seeking updates, a multitude of friends, family, and all those firemen—prompted one hospital official to pull Linda aside and politely tell her she would have to attempt to remedy the situation.

"Look, I'll try to keep everybody under control, but I'm *not* turning anybody away," Linda said through gritted teeth. "You can't fault Donny for having so many people who care about him."

AROUND MID-JANUARY, Dr. Posner decided to start weaning Donny off the ventilator, which by this time was pumping oxygen into him through a tracheotomy tube in his throat and not through his mouth, to reduce the damage to vocal cords and minimize the chance of infection. He cut back on the number of per-minute breaths the machine provided Donny, in the hopes that the patient might ultimately breathe on his own. Donny's heart and organs were functioning impressively, even if his brain was not.

"Let's see how he does," Dr. Posner said, explaining his respiratory game plan. And to the doctor's surprise and Linda's delight, Donny did remarkably well. After only a few days, he was breathing on his own.

By Friday, January 19, 1996, the three-week anniversary of the Inter Park roof collapse, Donny had survived without a single setback, problem, or infection. Linda's state, meanwhile, had gone from paralyzing shock to exhausted but brittle resiliency. The kids were doing okay, all things considered, though the older boys found it difficult to focus in school, at times crippled by the uncertainty.

Everyone missed Donny. His parents were shaken but unwilling to accept for even a moment that he would not recover to be anything other than the old Donny. Uncle Simon was torn apart. Childhood pal Bobby Bruenn and Donny's football buddies found themselves tortured by thoughts of Donny as a vegetable. But few men took the incident as hard as the firefighters of Rescue 1 and Engine 3, guys who were reminded every day of the void in the firehouse, and that it could have been any one of them.

Tragedy often triggers a unifying ripple effect, and the entire Buffalo community rallied around the Herberts. Plans for a major fund-raiser were already under way. So many people were calling and writing, all wondering how Donny was faring. Linda thought about issuing a statement to the local media. She had declined all interviews since the accident, but perhaps, she figured, doing one interview could ease the demand for information. One reporter for the *Buffalo News,* Gene Warner, had been calling Linda repeatedly, and his number was written down on a notebook on the kitchen table. Warner had at least always been polite, and the *News* was Buffalo's only major newspaper. So that Friday morning, Linda called Warner and invited him to the family's home on Durant Street, where they could talk in private.

In a front-page interview that was published the following Saturday under the headline "It's Going to Take a Miracle," Linda discussed Donny's condition and expressed her wish that everyone continue to keep Donny in their prayers.

"Whatever we get, we'll accept," Linda was quoted as saying. "I know it was a serious injury, but he didn't leave us that day for a reason. I know there's a purpose for him to be with us."

A SPECIAL HEALING MASS was held at St. Agatha's in early February. Many had suggested a larger church, such as the Our Lady of Victory Basilica or St. Joseph's Cathedral downtown, but Linda insisted that it be at tiny St. Agatha's. It was standing room only—hundreds of people from all over the city came, and a large crowd overflowed outside the church. Friends, firefighters, and strangers huddled just beyond the doors, undeterred by the cold.

A half dozen clergymen graced the altar, including Bishop Mansell, Monsignor Clody, Father Joe Bayne, Father Joe Moreno, and Father Robert Yetter, who until recently had been St. Agatha's pastor. Father Yetter led the Mass, and spoke of how amazed he was at the outpouring of support and prayers. Indeed, Linda and the boys had received by this time nearly eight hundred cards and notes, many of them, as it turned out, from elderly women promising to keep Donny in their thoughts and prayers.

As February wore on, Donny, still comatose yet not technically in a coma, began to exhibit some positive, albeit odd behavior. Once in a while, nurses reported to Linda, he would go through the motions of inserting what appeared to be an imaginary cigarette into his mouth, even raising his hand to light it, once going so far as to exhale an invisible puff of smoke. This reflexive compulsion of a heavy smoker didn't stun doctors, although observing it for herself Linda found it scary to watch. *What's going on in your head, Donny?* Some days, Donny would cough or hiccup. His eyes would open, but remained fixed, sometimes rolling back as if in a seizure.

Officially, one month after the roof collapse, ECMC listed Donny Herbert in fair condition, remarkable for a man who had not been expected to live. He appeared to hear sounds, to track them in his room, though he seemed to wince from the lights in the ICU. Donny could not speak, but in early February, when doctors removed the tracheotomy tube, he began to gurgle, what sounded like stunted attempts at speech. A speech therapist began trying to feed him soft food, Jell-O, mashed potatoes, but more often Donny ended up gagging, unable to swallow.

Linda, on the advice of her old friend Debbie Strzalkowski, a widowed nurse, had requested that Donny undergo a PET scan, a more in-depth reading of the brain than a CT scan, but it was never done. "There's nothing additional that a PET scan will tell us," one doctor told her, and Linda begrudgingly accepted the explanation. But the days of Linda simply taking at face value anything the doctors told her were running short.

She had to get more involved, ask more questions. This horrible ordeal had left her in her own kind of stupor during the past month, but she knew she had to snap out of it. She owed it to her family, to Donny.

Linda was determined to get her house in order, figuratively and literally. Her kitchen table was overrun by piles of unopened mail, bills, insurance forms, and of course, a growing stack of cards and letters. After the kids had gone to sleep, Linda poured herself a cup of tea and dove head-on into the paper mountain.

One of the first things she opened was a thick, oversized envelope from the photographer's studio where she and Donny and the boys had gathered for the family portrait on December 28—the last time Linda saw Donny before the tragedy. Flipping past the prints of the main portrait taken that day, Linda came to the ones of just their family, and staring down at them she felt as if she had been smacked in the face. Donny was missing.

AFTER SIX WEEKS in the ICU burn unit, Donny was moved into a rehabilitation wing for acute brain trauma patients. He was conscious but unresponsive. His eyes were open in waking hours. When prompted to undergo therapy, stretching his arms, standing with the help of a walker and a pair of nurse's aides, Donny would show some responsiveness, even if he could not complete the task and remained in his own dead-to-the-world fog. But he was alive, tracking sounds, making progress, slowly, steadily. Linda began to have some hope.

On February 16, Donny's rehab doctor, Maria Labi, sat down with Linda and several members of the Herbert family in an ECMC conference room. Dr. Labi had agreed to give them an update on Donny's condition and his chances of recovery. In a terse, don't-blame-the-messenger tone, Dr. Labi explained that despite the various signs of progress, the doctors still could not tell the true extent of Donny's brain damage, so therefore all they could do was continue with rehab and hope for the best. This didn't cut it, not with Linda.

What the doctor might have said, had the sit-down not been so emotionally fraught, was that in the world of traumatic brain injuries—of which there were more than one million each year in the United States alone— breakthroughs, apart from a handful of exceptions (such as the never-repeated L-dopa successes on encephalitis survivors with brain disorder symptoms similar to Parkinson's victims and famously heralded in the 1970s by Dr. Oliver Sacks of *Awakenings* notoriety) had not kept pace with the strides made in the treatment of a range of other medical maladies, such as cancer. And that despite scientific and technological advancements, treatment options for brain-damaged patients, save for continued stimulation therapy, different experimental meds, and time, were surprisingly few. That's what Dr. Labi might have said, not that it would have made much difference. But she'd gone with "We really just don't know," which was not exactly 100 percent accurate, but in the delicacy of the moment, it was the best she could offer and not all that far from the truth.

"That's it? That's all you can tell us?" Linda was growing frustrated. She was determined to stay in control, to stay on top of this situation. Her relationship with Donny's parents and sisters, never exceptionally cordial to begin with, became strained, which only added to the stress. Everyone on Donny's side of the family had strong opinions about what to do, setting the stage for a tug-of-war. But ultimately, what no one wanted to face, what was Linda's burden to bear, was that despite the progress he'd made, the odds of Donny's not getting better, of being in some vegetablelike condition for the rest of his life, were strong. Amid the murmurings of Donny's parents and sisters, Linda calmly pressed Dr. Labi for more information.

"Well, can you just give us some idea of what we are looking at, you know, in terms of the chances of Donny returning to the way he was before the accident?"

What Dr. Labi said next surprised everyone. She

replied that yes, there was still a chance that Donny could resume a normal life. "He may even be able to return to work in three months," she said.

Donny's parents were naturally encouraged to hear this; Linda found the statement borderline ludicrous.

"He's tough," Mr. Herbert declared. "I know my son can lick this."

Linda wasn't sure. She had to think realistically. Donny, after all, still wasn't even responsive. Everything she had read or learned thus far about anoxic brain injuries suggested that if improvements were to come—normally, if they came at all—they would come in the first three months. After that, the chances were practically zero.

Linda consulted with Simon, Donny's uncle, and Simon's wife, Kathy. They had just been through hell with their son Simon junior, who'd been diagnosed with a brain tumor. The boy was ultimately operated on and made a full recovery, but the experience taught Simon and Kathy that they needed to do their own independent research. First opinions and recommendations—even from esteemed practitioners—are invariably tainted by other circumstances, preconceived notions, inertia, and competing economic agendas. "You can't just sit back," Kathy advised.

A few days after the sit-down with Dr. Labi, Linda, on her own, met with an ECMC neurologist, Dr. Richard Cowan. Cowan agreed to review Donny's medical file. He examined Donny briefly and then offered a drastically more sobering prognosis.

"His condition is still very severe. If he makes it, most likely he will be severely brain damaged. And the longer he goes in this unresponsive state, the worse his chances are of ever returning to a level where he could function on his own."

Now Linda had two doctors offering up drastically different scenarios. She realized Simon and Kathy were right, that no matter what, from now on, she had to seek second and third opinions and not take anything for granted. She made her way over to the Dudley Public Library on South Park Avenue and looked up some old copies of *Consumer Reports,* trying to find special back issues with spotlights on the country's best hospitals. Kathy brought over a stack of information and spent hours walking Linda through some of the various steps involved, which inevitably led to Linda's firing off heartfelt letters to the Mayo Clinic, Johns Hopkins, and other well-known institutions. And every day, Linda continued to pray for some miracle that would bring Donny back.

People continued to come by the hospital to visit and show support, and the kids came after school almost every day. Donny's new room in the rehabilitation wing, on the eighth floor of ECMC, was tiny, and he shared it with another patient, or rather a rotating roster of patients in various levels of consciousness. Because Donny's room was often mobbed, Linda sometimes felt sorry for the patient in the other bed, lying there alone.

The rehab floor itself was crowded and noisy. A special gym was located several floors below. Here, every day, Donny underwent three excruciating hours of acute rehab—physical therapy, speech therapy, occupational therapy—with painfully slow results, tantamount to someone attempting to roust an impossibly drunk person into action. He could not form words. He could not stand on his own, but he seemed to be trying; neurons, at least some, anyway, were still interconnecting inside his brain, albeit dysfunctionally. At least there was some activity. When these sessions were over, Donny was propped up, listless, in a wheelchair in his room. Linda and the boys did their best to coax out the Donny they once knew but now could not reach.

On Tuesday, February 20, Monsignor Robert C. Wurtz, head of Our Lady of Victory Institutions and the third successor to the venerated Father Baker, made a surprise visit to Donny's room on the rehab wing. No one had asked him to come. Monsignor Wurtz had brought with him a crucifix that had once belonged to Father Baker. Holding it over Donny's head, Wurtz blessed him and just as quickly as he had come, proceeded to turn around and exit the room.

The following day, Ash Wednesday, another priest paid Donny an unexpected visit. This time it was Father Joseph Moreno (aka Father Cannoli), chaplain for the Buffalo Police Department. He knew Donny from their encounters at the scenes of accidents and tragedies, and felt compelled to come and administer him ashes, blessed and ritualistically smudged on his forehead in the sign of a cross.

INCREDIBLY, OVER THE NEXT several weeks in that late winter and early spring of 1996, Donny Herbert began to show marked improvement. First, his movements became more aggressive. He flailed, he grunted, as if he were physically fighting his way out of his trapped condition. He would pull out his feeding tube and try to get up from his bed.

He was slowly emerging and even seemed to recognize people, although doctors had discovered he was suffering from cortical blindness, a condition in which otherwise healthy, undamaged eyes are rendered useless because the neurological connections facilitating sight are not being made.

On February 29, Nicky asked his mom to write something for him in a sign-in book, on a table by the door. "You hugged me today and I sat on your lap. Thank you, Dad. Nick."

By early March Donny was able to stand up during

therapy and actually put one of his legs forward, a giant step for him in every sense. He would sometimes appear to sob when he came in contact with certain people, as if he could sense their heartbreak. But strange things were happening with more frequency. From the movements of his eyes and the grimacing expression, Donny appeared caught in a bizarre dreamlike state. Several people—nurses, his siblings—swore they heard Donny yelling for help.

Nine

ON MARCH 19, the feast of St. Joseph, Linda took Nicky to the Our Lady of Victory Basilica in Lackawanna. She lit a candle and prayed for Donny. Later that day, at ECMC, the nurses on the rehab wing were bursting. Donny spoke; one simple word, slurry but audible.

"Hi."

A few days later Donny was able to understand and deliver upon a therapist's instruction to produce a thumbs-up sign. He was able to answer when asked his age, "Thirty-four," but at the same time he appeared dreadfully woozy, almost punch-drunk. Still, he was beginning to come out of his comatose haze. For a man who was expected to die or be brain-dead, this level of recovery was surprising.

Donny could not initiate conversation. He struggled to get out even a few words. But he was *speaking*—his vocal cords were functioning. No one really knew what to expect going forward. Linda told herself that Donny would slowly but surely pull through.

More progress followed as the winter gave way to

spring. Donny's everyday reality was dominated by vivid awake "dreams," as his neurotransmitters fired and misfired simultaneously. Visitors who tried to communicate with him were met with curious mumblings, usually something about his sailing away on a ship.

Then, on other occasions, something—or rather *someone*—seemed to be trying to get him. Donny, who never showed fear before the accident, would recoil in horrified distress from his unseen tormentor.

One afternoon in late March, Linda sat Nicky on the edge of his father's hospital bed. Donny suddenly bolted up in a sitting position, swatting the boy with his powerful arm. Nicky, sent flying to the floor, began to wail hysterically.

"What the hell are you doing?!" Linda yelled at Donny.

Donny didn't react. He was clearly somewhere else, grumbling something that sounded like "Get away" as he kept flailing at an imaginary foe.

And Linda was flailing, too. She had put up with so much. She had held herself together bravely these past few months. But that day, when she saw her youngest beside himself and her husband lost in some frantic quasi-hallucination, she lost it, as if she, too, were trapped in a nightmare from which she could not wake.

ON GOOD FRIDAY, April 5, Nicky Herbert, in rubber gloves and an oversized surgeon's cap, walked into Donny's hospital room, tapped at his mother's leg, and informed her that they had a visitor.

"Mom, that bishop guy is here again."

Indeed, it was Bishop Mansell. He had come, unannounced, to bless Donny on this most sacred day of Holy Week, which culminated on Easter Sunday.

At the precise moment he walked into the room, Linda was already praying the Our Father at her husband's bedside. Donny, with an almost angelic torpor, eyes looking up to the heavens, loudly joined in. ". . . Thy kingdom come, thy will be done, on earth as it is in heaven. . . ."

The Bishop, slightly bewildered, prayed along with them. It was astonishing. To hear Donny speaking so clearly was shocking enough, but, eerily, Linda had never heard Donny's voice take on such a reverential tone; it was almost as if he had, for the moment, co-opted a beautiful singing voice to replace his gravelly, workingman's pipes.

When they all finished the prayer, Donny fell silent.

A WEEK OR SO LATER, Linda, for the first time since the accident, had to go to a major family event, a wedding, alone. She was certain it would be hard for her; it turned out to be more difficult than she had imagined.

The bride-to-be was Linda's younger sister, twenty-seven-year-old Jean. She was getting married to a good natured St. Martin's boy named Tom Finn, two years her senior. Tom's mother worked with Jean at Mercy Hospital and had fixed the two up a few years earlier. The ceremony was April 20 at St. Agatha's Church. Linda was in the wedding party. She did her best to be cheerful for her baby sister, the youngest of the seven girls, who had come over to Linda's house on Durant early that morning to start getting ready. But Linda was tired in every way, in her body, heart, and mind.

At the church, everyone asked how Donny was doing. Linda wasn't sure what to say. As much progress as Donny had made, he was still traveling (in his mind, sailing) on a long, difficult course: cortically blind, wheelchair-bound, and barely coherent. Everyone believed Donny would continue to get better; the alternative scenario, Donny stuck in this barely conscious, pathetic state, remained unfathomable to anyone who knew the man he once was. Always one to put on a brave front, Linda kept herself and others positive: "Donny is a fighter. If anyone can pull through, he can."

After the ceremony the wedding party made their way by rented trolley bus over to Cazenovia Park for photos. It was a gorgeously sunny spring day, the kind of spirit- and body-warming afternoon Buffalonians savor after an insultingly long winter.

When the photos were finished, newlyweds Jean and Tom insisted that the wedding party make a quick stop before heading off to the reception at a restaurant in West Seneca.

They all traveled up to ECMC to stop in and visit with Donny. He wasn't coherent, but he did manage to smile for a few photos, and in a small way was able to share with them in the happy event. A short while later, Donny mumbled something odd, barely intelligible, and to no one in particular. But Linda's sister Debbie heard him.

It was long ago and Donny was still sailing on that boat.

Ten

BUILT DOWNTOWN IN the late 1930s as part of FDR's Works Progress Administration, Buffalo Memorial Auditorium had played host to thousands of concerts and sporting events over the years, providing a fountain of magical moments and memories for generations.

In the 1940s, 1950s, and 1960s, "the Aud," as it came to be affectionately known, was a beehive of college basketball activity. The area's "Little Three"—Canisius College, Niagara University, and St. Bonaventure University—played top teams from around the country and drew legions of fans. In 1970, the Aud, which was originally designed to hold twelve thousand, expanded to accommodate around sixteen thousand fans, becoming the new home of the city's first NHL franchise, the Sabres, and, that same year, Buffalo's short-lived NBA team, the Braves.

At the end of the 1995–96 hockey season, the beloved Sabres moved into the larger, more luxurious Marine Midland Arena, a few blocks away. The Aud, antiquated and run-down, fell completely silent. Soon it would be closed for good. But on July 12, 1996, one final event would be held there: a benefit for Donny Herbert.

Organized by the local firefighters, the two-to-midnight party (to which admission was a twenty-dollar donation) attracted several thousand people and a lot of goodwill. People had fun; it was a party, after all. Huge pans of food and an ocean of beer, all donated, were trucked in. Linda's closest friends, Luanne and Terri, took care of the decorations—American flags, red-white-and-blue bunting, balloon archways. Mike Lombardo, Gary O'Neill, and some of the other firemen set up a silent auction table brimming with prizes—autographed jerseys, vacation packages, sporting goods, artwork, tickets, gift certificates—all donated. Proceeds would go toward Donny's care, most of which was being covered by the city, and some to a fund for the boys' educations. There would be bagpipers, rock bands, jazz bands, Irish step dancers all throughout the event.

Linda went to her Elmwood Avenue hairdresser that afternoon, knowing the media would be on hand for the party, and despite having put on some weight in the past several months, she was determined to look her best. She chatted with her stylist, Tony, about Donny's condition, openly and honestly, something she could not always do around the boys or others close to her. On the orders of Dr. Labi, Donny had been transferred a few days earlier from FCMC to the head trauma center at Our Lady of

Victory Hospital in Lackawanna, across the street from Father Baker's grand basilica. Although Donny had made some incredible strides, he still struggled with basic functions and spoke only when prodded. Progress, which for a while had been incremental but visible, appeared to be slowing.

Linda arrived at the benefit in a new floral print sundress. All her boys were already there ahead of time, and volunteers were setting up. Linda looked around. She could not believe the last event ever to be held at the Aud was going to be a benefit for her husband. All those winter nights she'd spent at the concession stand selling ice cream and soda, working happily alongside her sisters, and with Donny. Those were the days.

Linda and the boys mingled with people they knew and met many others they did not, dozens of Buffalonians who felt compelled to introduce themselves. Donny had touched more lives than Linda and the boys had even realized.

At about seven P.M. a hush came over the crowded auditorium as Donny, flanked by Linda and the kids, was brought up on a small stage. Dave Donnelly, president of the firefighters union, joined the family onstage. Donny sat awkwardly in his wheelchair, withdrawn, gaunt. For some people it was the first time they had seen him, which was difficult. Many began to cry. Nicky, wearing the cutest little tuxedo, leaned on his dad's lap, looking up at him proudly. Linda, hovering over Donny's right shoulder, whispered in his ear, conveying as best she could everything that was going on. Donny seemed only partially there. He wasn't talking, but he did appear to be listening.

Taking the microphone, Donnelly read out a Common Council proclamation officially declaring July 12, 1996, "Donald Herbert Day" as the crowd burst into applause. Linda surveyed the scene, all those faces; loved ones, friends, neighbors, and strangers. Young mothers and South Buffalo firemen alike were teary eyed. When Linda leaned in close to kiss her husband on the cheek, she noticed that Donny had begun to cry, too.

AS THE SUMMER WORE ON, though, Donny gradually began to slip farther and farther away. Linda and the boys did their best to carry on as normally as they could under the circumstances, remaining hopeful that somehow things would turn around. They braced themselves for special occasions, crushing reminders of the way life used to be for them, before the accident. Already they had endured Tommy's eighth-grade graduation, Father's Day, and Don junior's fifteenth birthday, with each occasion stirring up painful emotions. In August, they had suffered through Tommy's fourteenth birthday. Linda and the kids gathered around the table blowing out candles, while Donny was lying up at OLV in his stupor. People would tell Linda that she needed to get through these first few milestones, and then they would start to get easier. Linda found the opposite was true. While she was doing her best to keep Donny connected to his family, the fact that he was missing out on so much tore away at her. Tommy, the best athlete of the bunch, was heading off to Timon, and Donny, who would have been so proud, was oblivious. Nicky had set out for his first day of school, and Donny hadn't been there to see his little buddy off. Life was going by, and Donny was missing it.

People could have written Donny off, resumed their routines. It had been almost a year. But from friends and family to the loyal brethren on the BFD, no one ever did. Visitors still poured in. Donny's parents kept a vigil by his bedside every day. Sometimes Don junior and Tommy would go right to Donny's room after Timon soccer practice, to tell him of their victories and defeats. Because the OLV head-trauma facility was right across the street from the basilica, many of Donny's visitors used the opportunity to stop by and say a special prayer to Father Baker. Sometimes Donny's mom or an old friend would ask permission from Monsignor Wurtz to pray upon a relic of the venerated priest, like the crucifix or a vestment that belonged to him, which were kept locked in his shrine on the ground floor of the magnificent church. Wurtz obliged as many of these requests as he could. Joe Corey, a former Baker-Victory gym teacher who lived nearby the hospital and who had never forgotten Donny Herbert, was battling his own demon, neck cancer. He'd been given only three months to live. Corey, when he had the strength, would lurch, gasping, to Donny's room, using the visits as inspirational sessions, praying to Father Baker for both of their recoveries.

Corey, amazingly, did get better. Donny, on the other hand, appeared to be fading away, creeping farther and farther into the vegetative state Linda and the children had so feared.

Dr. Labi was trying different medications on Donny, but from Linda's perspective it was not clear what was being administered. Whatever the case, the medicines produced various side effects. Some days he would spend abnormally lengthy periods awake, often twenty hours or more, marked by fits of shaking, followed by intensely long periods of sleep. But there was no real improvement. While the head-trauma unit at Our Lady of Victory had been billed by the ECMC doctors as a uniquely suited facility for Donny to continue with subacute rehab and, possibly, the next step to getting him home, Linda realized soon enough that this special unit at OLV was basically just another hospital wing filled with other catatonic or coma-like brain-injury patients. Donny still was not walking, unless one counted taking a few steps with the help of a walker and two rehab nurses with a wheelchair directly behind him. He required a feeding tube. Further attempts to feed him soft food were abandoned for fear that Donny might aspirate. He was still unable to control that most basic of functions most people take for granted: swallowing. He could not control his bladder or bowels. He could not say who he was, nor where he was, nor anything really at all. Eventually, Donny stopped talking altogether. He sat in his wheelchair, head hanging down, tired, so tired, like a man who hadn't slept in years.

In October of 1996, Dr. Labi suggested that Donny undergo surgery to place a shunt in his brain to relieve pressure believed to be hindering his recovery, but the procedure had no effect.

Linda, knowing the crucial recovery window for patients like Donny was closing fast, pinned her hopes on one of the major medical facilities, such as the Mayo Clinc. Unfortunately, none of them would accept Donny. Administrators explained in formally phrased letters that based on his records, there was little else they felt they could do beyond the treatment that was already being provided. But in Linda's opinion that was unacceptable.

Around Thanksgiving, Simon suggested that Linda take Donny to the Lake Erie Institute of Rehabilitation, about ninety minutes south of Buffalo in Erie, Pennsylvania, for a second opinion. Linda studied up further and learned that LEIR was considered to be one of the better programs in the country for Donny's type of injury. And here it was, practically right in their backyard. Linda put the wheels in motion, despite a less than enthusiastic reaction from Dr. Labi, not to mention the vociferous objections of Donny's parents, who expressly did not want their beloved son to be moved so far away. Donny's mother, Geraldine, had been as rattled as anyone by his ordeal. She could not bear the harsh reality of what had happened to her pride and joy. Linda knew Geraldine was hurting—everyone was hurting—and she tried her best to calmly explain her rationale for taking Donny to Erie. Around-the-clock care from a highly skilled staff was Donny's best shot at a return to normalcy. They at least had to try.

Linda was second-guessed by Donny's side of the family, at times even accused, either behind her back or by way of insinuation, of wanting to shunt Donny away, out of sight. Tension built. Sides were invariably taken. Many of those closest to Donny, including Uncle Simon, Bobby Bruenn, and Father Joe Bayne, found themselves caught in the middle.

But Linda felt she had no other choice and vowed never again to explain her motives where Donny was concerned. Let them whisper or scoff behind her back. She had four active boys to raise, and a husband to try to rescue.

ON FEBRUARY 10, 1997, Donny was discharged from the head-trauma unit of Our Lady of Victory Hospital in Lackawanna and transported to the Lake Erie Institute of Rehabilitation in Erie, Pennsylvania. Of course, it wasn't quite that simple. Upon admission to LEIR, a routine examination found Donny to be dehydrated and running a fever. Doctors suspected he was suffering from pneumonia.

Instead of taking up residency at the rehab facility, Donny was rushed across the street to Hamot Medical Center and put into isolation. Days later, when his vitals improved sufficiently, he was permitted to be formally admitted to his new home away from home.

After a few more days of rest, Donny began intensive therapy. Some days he was in better spirits than others. In terms of physical fitness, Donny was still a lot stronger than most other people. And it was apparent that deep inside, Donny's competitive fires were still burning.

Linda adjusted to her new routine, rising early, seeing the kids off to school, going to work as a crossing guard for an hour, then making the long drive to the institute, usually getting there by around eleven-thirty A.M. Nicky spent the mornings at a preschool program offered at Southside High School. In the afternoon, Linda's dad playfully appointed the little boy part of his custodial staff at Southside, issuing him his very own putty knife for gum-scraping detail. Nicky loved it.

If Linda made the trip out to Erie in the late morning, she would drive back to be home in time to pick Nicky up at four P.M., and then make dinner for the boys. On other days, if she went to Erie after school, she would bring Nicky along, and any of the other boys who could join them. Patrick, in seventh grade at St. Agatha's, was always eager to go. Tommy and Don junior were often busy with soccer practice, but truth be told, they had each found the trip difficult. Some nights, everybody went together They could get there by five-thirty P.M. and catch a meal before the cafeteria closed. If Linda left by seven-thirty P.M., she could make it home in time to get the kids in bed at a decent hour, often driving in the dark, through snow squalls on slippery roads. A lot of Donny's friends from the department made the trip to Erie that winter and spring, as did a few fellows from the Cleveland Fire Department who had heard about Donny Herbert.

One spring day, the weather having turned warmer, Linda tried to do something special—take Donny and Nicky to the Erie Zoo. She'd called up a handicap-friendly van service to come get them at the LEIR facility. The impending outing had her feeling cheerful, a lot more upbeat than she had been in weeks. The moment was fleeting.

For openers, when it came time to load Donny into the back of the van, the driver appeared hesitant to operate the hydraulic lift, almost uncomfortable. But they managed together to strap Donny in as best they could and took off for the zoo. The midmorning sun beat down on the zoo's asphalt sidewalks. It had been brisk earlier in the day when they left, but the zoo was now oppressively hot. Worse, it was hilly. Linda struggled to push Donny's cumbersome wheelchair up the hills; going downhill required an even greater degree of agility, the dull wheels swiveling helter-skelter, seemingly with a will of their own.

Then Nicky had to go to the bathroom. Linda did not want to send the boy into the men's room alone, nor could she leave Donny outside unattended. Did she bring the both of them into the ladies' room with her? She was grasping for answers and decided to send Nicky in by himself.

Charged with a helpless adult in a wheelchair and a five-year-old child, strapped with a purse and a duffel bag filled with Donny's things—feeding tube, meds, water, a towel, adult diapers—Linda opted to herd her party onto a sight-seeing train she had noticed when they first arrived. The train, which snaked around the entire zoo, was a perfect solution. Fortuitously, it had a wheelchair lift. Drenched in sweat, Linda took a gulp from the water bottle. Her achy body was loving that seat, and the thought of ever getting up seemed impossible. That's when Linda decided that they would simply stay on the train—all day. They would sit there, going around and around, until it was time to go back.

Linda caught her breath and relaxed. She pointed out some camels to Nicky. At long last, a badly needed moment of peace, one that lasted all of a few minutes. Donny was wearing a Buffalo Fire Department baseball cap. From out of the blue, a gust of wind came and blew it off his head, carrying it down into a ravine.

Beyond distraught, Nicky started to howl. "Dad's hat! We have to get Dad's hat!"

Rarely one to throw fits or tantrums, Nicky broke from character now. He would not let up. That hat, getting it back, was life or death to him. To calm him down, Linda promised, swore, they would find it. Of course, the spot where the hat blew away was miles from where the train had let them off. But they circled back, slogging to the ravine.

Good God, what am I doing?

In a split-second decision, Linda dashed off, leaving Nicky to watch his father. Linda half slid down the steep embankment on her backside, carefully, so as not to slip or twist an ankle, then scurried across the train tracks to where she hoped the hat would be. Frantically, she looked all around, but didn't see it anywhere. Here she was, in this ominous ravine, negotiating the train tracks and the sharp brush, panicked that a train would come by or a zoo official might radio security, nervous over not knowing what was happening up above with Nicky and his father, and here *that stupid fucking hat* was nowhere to be found.

Please. I know I've asked for a lot this past year. I can accept what's happened to Donny, I accept all of this. I haven't lost my faith in you. But I pray to you now. Please, please let me find this baseball hat.

Thank God, Linda would tell her boys later, for answered prayers.

Eleven

AFTER THE FIASCO at the zoo, Linda limited Donny and Nicky's outdoor time together to a sitting area at a Lake Erie marina connected by a walkway to the grounds of the rehab institute. Nicky liked to watch the boats. Donny was lost somewhere, perhaps sailing on a vessel of his own. Since being injured back on that cold morning, he had been comatose, semiconscious, borderline lucid, less lucid, and now seemed stuck in what the doctors referred to as a "minimally conscious state."

Although Donny was getting the rehab he needed—occupational, physical, speech, social stimulation—he did not improve during the long summer of 1997. He was working hard, or at least appeared to be, struggling through agonizing sessions where it seemed his limbs were made of concrete. The doctors would alter his meds and look for some changes, but there was little progress. His only response, from time to time, was a barely discernible thumbs-up sign he *might* give, if coaxed.

These were heartbreaking months. Sometimes Linda could not bear her own thoughts. All along, she had held out hope that Donny would leave LEIR well enough, improved enough, to return to their family home. Lately, though, the doctors were increasingly suggesting that she think about finding skilled, twenty-four-hour care providers in Buffalo. There was not much more that they could do for him in Erie. She hated to cry in public, but these conversations caused her to well up every time.

Daily, Linda grappled with an imaginary viewpoint: what Donny would have wanted. Well, he certainly would not want to live in a nursing home. Who would? On the other hand, with Donny, the kids always came first. What kind of upbringing could the boys hope to have with their father hovering about in a helpless stupor? Would their friends ever feel comfortable coming over? Linda tried to imagine them doing homework, watching TV, or listening to music with a visiting nurse changing and cleaning their father in the next room. It was hard enough for the boys to even visit him.

Only Nicky seemed not to mind—but the older kids had more memories of Donny, more pain to stomach. Linda had once told her eldest boys that it would take all three of them to equal one of their dad, and that raising Nicky was going to require all of their help. Yet Nicky was extremely well-adjusted, and in his naive way seemed to be doing the best of everyone. But for how much longer? Such a painful daily reminder would be too much for any child to cope with.

Don junior had the hardest time of all. To numb the pain he started partying a little too much, although Linda promptly nipped that in the bud. Tommy and Patrick were stoic, but it was tough on them, too. They often found themselves fighting back tears. But their involvement in sports proved to be a healthy diversion, and they always tried to maintain a positive attitude.

But even if the boys could adjust, even if Linda brought Donny home regardless and cared for him nonstop, realistically, could she manage it and still find time to give her boys what they needed as well?

Meanwhile, Donny's mother and father were convinced that they were best suited and more than happy to take care of Donny in his childhood home on Melrose Street. They argued their point by saying that that was what their son would have wanted. But Linda reached a different conclusion.

She had prayed for a miracle. It didn't come. She had given her husband the highest-quality rehab she could find (and that the City of Buffalo would agree to pay for), and Donny's condition had only gotten worse. Back on the morning of Donny's injury, Linda had prayed to God not to take him from her, no matter what. At that time she didn't exactly know what "no matter what" might mean.

Now she did. In the hardest decision of her life, Linda chose to place Donny in a convalescent home in Buffalo. That September she began to look.

Armed with a computer printout list of nursing homes within a fifty-mile radius of South Buffalo, Linda drove around with Donny's patient advocate from LEIR, shooting from one place to the next, circumnavigating Buffalo's first-ring suburbs, from Amherst and Tonawanda in the north to Cheektowaga in the southeast. She even went as far as East Aurora, almost forty minutes away, to visit a home called the Waters of Aurora Park, but pleasant as it was, to Linda it somehow just didn't feel right. Linda agreed to visit one more, Father Baker Manor.

Operated by the Catholic Health System, Father Baker Manor had started out as yet another facility in a long line of Our Lady of Victory institutions going back to the old iron-barred orphanage. It was only a few years old, nicely laid out, and clean. Right away, Linda had a good feeling about it. The one-story home sat on leafy grounds, set back off a rural road in Orchard Park, near Chestnut Ridge. Most important, Father Baker Manor was not too far from South Buffalo (a mere fifteen-minute shot up the 219). The rooms were large and offered more privacy than some of the others Linda had seen. At the main entrance there hung a beautiful framed portrait of the diminutive, kindly Father Baker, rather Harry Truman–esque and clad in his black monsignor's garb and tasseled hat, a peaceful sentry on perpetual watch. To Linda, the patients at this home seemed to be better cared for, and the staff seemed friendlier.

As she walked the hallways she heard a familiar voice. "Linda?"

She looked over to see an old neighbor, Berta Duringer, the girl from Good Avenue who had been orphaned at a young age along with her seven siblings. Berta, always a rock, wore a comforting smile on her face.

"Linda . . . is that you?"

"Hey, Berta," Linda said. "It's great to see you!"

"What are you doing here?"

Linda wondered the same thing about Berta, who, it turned out, worked at Father Baker Manor in an administrative position. Linda began with some awkwardness to explain why she was there. Berta could see that Linda needed some reassurance, which she gave with the warmth and sincerity only a long-lost friend from the neighborhood could have dispensed at that moment.

"He'll like it here," Berta said. "This is a good place."

LINDA WAS DETERMINED to be both mother and father to her four boys. They would not miss out on a thing. She would make sure they had rides to practices. She attended every one of their games. She still took them camping. At Christmas they kept up tradition by going out into the countryside to cut down a tree.

In the autumn of 1997, Donny settled into his new life at Father Baker Manor. His room, 403, was the last one on the right, in the rear of the facility, with a window overlooking a loading dock. Donny's wing, or "neighborhood," as the nursing home staff preferred to call it, was known as Sterling Court. In the mornings, Donny would "wake" around ten A.M., although from the time he set foot in Father Baker Manor he was completely unresponsive. The nurses would give him his nourishment, fluids, and meds—vitamins, stool softeners—through his PEG tube. Then they would wash his face with a damp cloth, brush his thinning hair, and finally, get him dressed for the day in a BFD sweatshirt and sweatpants.

Every day, with the help of two aides and a walker, the rehab nurses did their best to force Donny to go for a walk. Even a few steps, just down the hall and back again, could take an hour, but it was important for overall physical stimulation. Donny usually had some visitors: Linda; his mom and dad, brothers and sisters; guys from the firehouse; old football buddies. He always took an afternoon nap at the insistence of the nurses. He had an entire team at his disposal: a general physician assigned to his wing; a dentist; a podiatrist; a full-time social worker, Patricia Fernandes, who served as his advocate and liaison with the family; a team coordinator, nurse Lynn Hornberger, who supervised the various therapists. There were also nurse's aides, orderlies, and rehab specialists across three shifts, all of whom interacted with Donny in some way. Now and again a group of Southtowns High School students taking part in a local Board of Cooperative Educational Services (BOCES) occupational health-care program would come in to provide assistance as part of their coursework. They were supervised, entrusted with only small tasks, such as clipping Donny's nails or shaving him. Because of his unresponsive state, Donny made for an ideal training patient, and the kids were good to him.

As part of the holistic community environment fostered by Father Baker Manor, Donny attended different social activities, such as weekly bingo (although he really didn't take part so much as sit there, indifferent, while Linda or one of the nurse's assistants marked his card for him). On Friday afternoons he attended Mass in the Father Baker chapel, normally with his dad. Sometimes people in the chapel swore that they had heard Donny humming along to a hymn or noticed him mouthing the words to the Our Father.

From the moment Donny entered Father Baker Manor, his parents had tried to petition the courts for legal guardianship of him, so strong was their objection to his being placed in a nursing home. But they visited him every day. Linda made sure that her schedule and Geraldine's rarely coincided, such was the contentious nature of their feud.

After everything Linda had been through during the

past two years, having to jump through legal hoops to prove Donny's "alleged incapacitation" and to establish her legal right to make decisions on his behalf was the absolute last thing she'd wanted to deal with, although with pro bono assistance from Uncle Simon she fought the case successfully.

During the winter of 1998, Linda was down in Florida visiting her uncle John and aunt Kay, who by this time had a spare room for her and had long since done away with the clumsy foldout couch. There she heard about a legal case similar to her own. One of her cousin Cathy's coworkers, Mike, a male nurse about the same age as Linda and Donny, was having an epic legal battle with his in-laws over the guardianship of his wife, who'd been in a persistent vegetative state since collapsing from cardiac arrest in 1990. Just as in Linda's situation, his relationship with his spouse's parents had grown particularly contentious after he placed a procedural Do Not Resuscitate order on his wife's medical chart. A state judge had ruled against the parents' bid for guardianship. Linda felt slightly comforted, knowing that she was not alone in her ordeal.

Later on, Linda would learn much more about this Florida case in the media. So would the rest of the world. Mike, the nurse who had worked alongside Linda's cousin in St. Pete, was Michael Schiavo; his wife was Terri.

Now it was up to Linda to make Donny proud, and that meant making sure the boys grew up into fine, upstanding young men. Every day was a struggle for her. Just getting out of bed could be a trial. She continued to hope for a miracle and to seek out the best medical treatment she could find, but they had to carry on as a family.

With the help of some of the money raised at the July 1996 benefit for Donny, as well as the generosity of family and friends, Linda was able to keep her three eldest enrolled at Bishop Timon. All of them were outstanding on the soccer field. Don junior, the always-well-positioned defender, and Tommy, a one-man offensive juggernaut, played together on the varsity team, while Patrick excelled on the junior varsity team.

She also decided to sell the property at 90 Spaulding— that old house she and Donny had bought from Bessie Cummings. Linda then bought a much larger house on the corner of McKinley Parkway and Abbott Road, not far from the Buffalo Irish Center. The neighborhood was still part of St. Agatha's Parish, but it was a landmark move. By a distance of about one-quarter mile, Linda would now be dwelling farther from her childhood home than she ever had before.

Buying the bigger house on McKinley made sense on paper. She could then rent out the Durant Street home to cover the monthly mortgage. Besides, they needed more room for Donny's visits. In the new house, Donny would have his own spacious quarters where visiting nurses could privately tend to his needs. Linda had a ramp and a wheelchair lift installed. The two eldest boys each had their own rooms. The youngest, Nicky and Patrick, shared a room upstairs, which by itself was almost as large as the entire house on Durant.

The days and weeks went by. Linda and the boys got along the best they could. After working as a crossing guard and putting in a load of wash, Linda would shoot out to Father Baker. She'd sit with Donny and tell him about the boys. Although she knew he didn't hear or understand her, it still felt right to keep talking to him as if he did. When the Timon soccer team dramatically defeated St. Joe's in the semifinals, 1–0 in overtime, it was Tommy who scored the winning goal. Don junior was getting all 90s on his report cards and was planning on going away to college on a partial scholarship. Neither Donny nor Linda had so much as contemplated going to college. Linda ached over Donny's inability to share her pride in their boys.

On days when Linda didn't feel talkative, they'd sit and watch *All My Children* together, sometimes the whole Channel 7 lineup, straight through to *General Hospital*. "If you ever do wake up, Donny, at least you'll be caught up on your soaps," Linda would joke.

Sometimes Linda shut the door, closed the blinds, grabbed a quilt, and just sacked out in the recliner next to

Donny's bed. *You're napping now, so I may as well catch one. That's what we'll do, Don, we'll take naps together.*

Or sometimes Linda would just stare out the window and watch life at Father Baker Manor go by. Donny's room on Sterling Court was a hideaway, like that far-flung table in a restaurant, the one that's practically part of the kitchen. Linda preferred being out of the way, appreciated the privacy.

The room's proximity to the rear of the facility provided Linda with an unfettered glimpse into the various inner workings of FBM, whether by overhearing the random gossip of orderlies on cigarette breaks or by simply watching the assorted unloadings and pickups—garbage, dirty linens, expired residents. Whenever the hearse pulled up, Linda got the creeps.

Most days, Linda would leave Father Baker's in time to run some errands, come home, and make dinner for whoever was hungry, then see that the boys had rides to practices, games, or wherever else they needed to go. She never wanted the boys coming home to an empty house. She spent most afternoons shuttling the boys back and forth between soccer, football, and baseball games. In the evening she saw to it that they did their homework. She fixed them snacks, allowed them a few hours of television, and got them to bed, usually by 11 P.M. In the calm of night Linda did housework. For someone who had previously spent entire days on the couch snoozing or watching talk shows, Linda, in those first few years after the accident, probably did not sleep more than a few full nights, getting by mainly on catnaps, Donny-style, five uninterrupted minutes between dishes, wash, more wash, paying bills, signing permission slips, and helping one of the kids sell something—candy bars, holiday decorations—to raise money for school. There was always some money due somewhere. Sometimes unfolded laundry piled up, but Linda made sure there was food in the house, clean clothes for the boys. She made sure they were active in sports, anything they wanted to do. Donny could not make their games, but she made damn sure she did. Nicky was dragged from practice field to gymnasium, possibly becoming the best known first grader in South Buffalo. "Hi, Nicky," or "Hey, little Herby!" could often be heard shouted from all directions, it seemed, wherever he went.

She and the kids subsisted like this for years. When Donny did come home to visit—not as often as Linda had originally envisioned, but a few times a month—the kids would try to spend some time with him, but inevitably, they retreated uncomfortably to their rooms. It was just too much.

Unpaid bills were piling up, and while Linda still collected Donny's paycheck—in the eyes of the Buffalo Fire Department, he was never taken out of service—the family had always relied upon his numerous side gigs to get by. There were medical expenses not covered by the city or the long-tapped kitty of benefit money, not to mention legal bills from her attempt to sue the absentee owners of the Inter Park property for violating the building code, which ultimately resulted in a modest settlement.

With money tight, Linda was presented with a major financial decision in the summer of 2000: sell one home, live in the other. Linda's sister Jean and her husband, Tom Finn, had been renting Linda's old house on Durant Street all these years. However, they had recently had a second child, Colleen, and now a third was on the way. And so they began to look for a home of their own. Linda's choice became easy. She and the boys would move back to Durant. Although the home on McKinley was much bigger, all the extra space seemed to make it a little too easy for the boys to withdraw to their rooms.

Plus, without Donny, the house on McKinley was never a *home*.

Twelve

ONE SUMMER DAY Linda thought it would be a good idea to take the boys camping. It was important for the family to do the things they used to enjoy together. Linda knew that with Don junior soon heading off to college, the time for this kind of excursion was running out.

So they packed up Linda's Ford Explorer (with Donny not there to insist on the secondhand wagon rule, she had splurged) and set out for Arrowhead, a small, family-owned campground in Delevan, New York, about fifty miles south of Buffalo, not too far from a speck of a city called Olean. They'd been going there for years. Dick and Diane Bull ran the place with their three kids. Dick let Linda have first dibs on the most secluded spot, the family favorite, out in the back meadow by the stream. Every site had a picnic table and a fire pit. Because it was set so far off from the main restroom facility, this one also had an outhouse. Nearby, there was a decent-sized pond for swimming and fishing, though in all these years no one, not even Patrick, ever caught much of anything.

Linda had planned this trip for days—and was exceptionally prepared. She'd packed all the essentials: flashlights and matches, lighter fluid, charcoal, an ax, canned goods, bug spray, sleeping bags, extra blankets, clothes, ice and a cooler, chips, soda, jugs of water, fishing poles, tackle, Frisbees, folding chairs, a football—they were set for three days, easy.

As Linda pulled up to the site, the August skies above were threatening. The boys began to unload the back of the Explorer, not exactly jumping for joy but open to the idea of one last great camping adventure together. Linda had a strange feeling that she'd forgotten something but couldn't quite place what. They'd figure it out, or better yet, hopefully not even notice or need whatever it was.

The cold droplets of rain were just starting to make themselves known. "This will blow over," Linda told the boys. "We can ride it out in the tent. Hey, then maybe we'll go for a hike or do some fishing. Come on, the quicker we get set up, the more time we'll have before it gets dark."

That's when Linda realized what she had forgotten. *She'd forgotten the damn tent!* She had two choices: pack everything up and call it a day, or do what Donny would have done—persevere.

Linda placed Don junior in charge and hopped back in the Explorer. Storm clouds were rumbling as she sped off. She proceeded to drive straight back home, forty-five minutes, pick up the tent from where it was sitting in the back-yard, and then turn around and head back to Arrowhead. When she arrived it was pouring rain. The boys were crouched under a tree, having stacked all the supplies under the picnic table. At least they hadn't been struck by lightning.

While it wasn't easy to orchestrate under the dark and drizzly nightfall, Linda and the boys did successfully pitch the tent, and later on started a fire. Not the best fire, mind you; there wasn't much dry wood to be found. Certainly, it was nothing like the blazes Donny used to produce, the kind of campfire where you had to move your chair back it was so hot. No, the boys had to work on it, feed it, prod it through the night, merely to keep it going. But keep it going they did. At least long enough to cook up some hot dogs and s'mores.

Zipped snugly in a damp sleeping bag, rocks nudging her shoulders, Linda listened to her four boys snoring away under the stars. She took a deep breath. She liked the smell of the old musty tent. She liked that they'd survived.

THE ROMAN CONGREGATIONS are the Catholic Church's formal administrative bodies, each headed up by a cardinal, almost like papal cabinet secretaries. There's a congregation for clergy and one for bishops, one for sacraments and another for doctrine. And one is charged with the canonization process: the Congregation for the Causes of Saints.

In the spring of 2001, the congregation dispatched a tribunal to western New York. The mission was straightforward but sensitive. They were to gather information on Father Nelson H. Baker, his life, his works, and most important, his supporters' claims of authentic "miracles." To be probed were several stories of remarkable occurrences involving supposed intercession. Only one year earlier, such an occurrence had garnered significant notoriety and the keen attention of Buffalo's Catholic leaders, Bishop Mansell and Monsignor Wurtz, the latter of whom was leading the Father Baker canonization effort.

The episode involved a terminally ill sixteen-year-old boy named Joseph Donohue III. During a horrific bout with bacterial meningitis in the intensive care unit of Buffalo Children's Hospital, Donohue was induced into a coma and hooked up to life support. His eye sockets ran red with blood. His body blackened like a piece of rotting fruit. Even if he lived, his limbs would most likely have to be amputated. But doctors gave him very little chance of survival. His parents, on the suggestion of a priest from Most Precious Blood in Buffalo, prayed for a Father Baker miracle. A piece of cloth from a vestment worn by Father Baker had been placed upon the sick boy, as was dirt said to be from the holy man's original gravesite. A few days later, to the amazement of the attending nurses and physicians, Donohue staged a full recovery.

Furthermore, when he woke from the coma, the young man recounted a dream he'd had while asleep. In the dream, he saw Father Baker.

While details of this story were widely reported in the local media, the incident was never presented to the Vatican's congregation by Monsignor Wurtz because the family never came forth voluntarily, a Vatican stipulation. But it was in actuality *another* supposed miraculous occurrence that specifically prompted their momentous visit to the Buffalo area. Two years earlier, Father Baker's body had been removed from his resting place in Holy Cross Cemetery. This order had come down from the Vatican, through Bishop Mansell, so that the iconic priest's remains might be reinterred in a tomb within the Basilica of Our Lady of Victory. The rationale for the move was that more people could come and pay their respects and pray to him, raising his profile, and thus perhaps even strengthening the cause for his canonization. Bishop Mansell oversaw the exhumation. On the day it was scheduled, a crowd of pilgrims and curious devotees gathered. When Father Baker's grave was opened, a separate vault was unearthed on top of the one that contained his remains. This smaller vault held three vials. Inside each of the vials was blood believed to have been drained from Father Baker's body at the time of his embalming.

As if the discovery of the secret vault and the mysterious vials had not been baffling enough, it was later learned that the fluid in the containers, rubber-corked glass, had somehow remained in pristine condition. How, the bishop and other clergymen on hand wondered, could human blood remain in liquid form after more than sixty years?

The vials were sent to the Vatican and tested. Congregation tribunal officials came to take sworn testimony from those involved in the process of reinterring Father Baker. More and more, it was looking to Monsignor Wurtz that somehow this bizarre finding—Father Baker's incorruptible blood—could be the first of the two miracles required for him to be canonized a saint. And at that point, God, the Vatican, and the Congregation for the Causes of Saints willing, he would need but one more.

Thirteen

DESPITE ALL OF the medical treatments, drugs, therapies, consultations, and examinations; despite an unrivaled physical fortitude that many had assumed would carry him through; despite infinite faith and support on the part of Linda and the boys; despite the hopes, wishes, and prayers of thousands upon thousands of friends and strangers; despite all of this, Donny Herbert did not get better. He got worse.

Doctors could quibble over whether Donny was in a "minimally conscious state" or in a "persistent vegetative state." It didn't matter. For anyone who knew Donny, the agonizing, harsh reality of what he had become defied clinical description. The man in the wheelchair, with his head slumped over, was an abomination. It was not Donny Herbert.

DAYS UNFOLDED, one after the other, without Donny Herbert. He was a trillion miles away from it all.

Donny's father died. The handicap van took him to the

funeral parlor while Patrick waited outside. Donny had no idea.

The attacks of September 11 occurred, and Donny was none the wiser. Everybody said the same thing: Donny would have been there—he would have gone to Ground Zero to help with search and rescue.

That December, the city so famous for its harsh winter weather endured a three-day snowstorm to rival the devastating Blizzard of '77. When all was said and done, certain areas of Buffalo had been buried by more than *seven feet* of snow. People were digging out for days. Donny would have been shoveling around the clock.

Meanwhile, Buffalo had fallen into financial disarray, with a state-authorized control board seizing the city's purse strings. Every civil servant from teacher to sanitation worker was put on notice that his or her job could be in jeopardy. Donny would have been fighting for the rights of the members of the Buffalo Professional Firefighters Local 282, whatever he could do, gathering signatures on petitions, working the political back channels. There weren't too many people who couldn't say they owed Donny Herbert a favor.

The Herbert boys, meanwhile, were doing superbly. Nicky earned good grades, played sports, and appeared to be a happy kid with none of the residual emotional baggage that might have come from growing up with such a trauma.

Husky Patrick, a shot put stalwart on the Timon track

and field team, ended up losing a good deal of weight toward the end of high school, stealthily growing into a handsome young man. He was a good kid, too, who never complained over the years when his mom asked him to help fold laundry or fix something around the house. Without having to be asked, he always looked after his little brother, Nicky.

In a way Patrick's whole life was based around a single question: *What would my dad think?* In the summer before his senior year at Timon, Patrick, in what was part tribute to Donny and partly a challenge to himself to get in better shape, went out for the varsity football team. Coach Fitzpatrick normally didn't take too warmly to latecomer walk-ons who had never played organized ball, but when he heard of Patrick's intentions, he was open to the idea. And while Patrick didn't start—in fact, all season he played only a few snaps as third-string defensive lineman— he had proven to himself he could hack it.

Tommy—who in his senior year at Timon had been named the school's Athlete of the Year on account of his being All-Catholic in soccer, cross-country, and track— went on to the University of Buffalo, where he became a standout on the rugby field, eventually leading a western New York squad to glory in the Empire State Games.

Don junior became a true adventurer. During the first semester of his senior year at Alfred University, he'd gone off to study in southwest China as part of a program offered by the School for International Training, based in Brattleboro, Vermont. Living in the rural regions of the Yunan Province, Don junior couldn't have been farther away from South Buffalo, from the bad memories, from the very name *Don Herbert* he shared with his father, and the associations it evoked. He learned that China had almost forty separate cultural groups, Tibetans, Mongolians, many peoples he'd never heard of. During his college years, Don, an anthropology major, had become quite bookish, delving into poetry, theology, and philosophy, although he wasn't averse to history or science binges. Don junior's dream was one day to travel to Tibet and the Himalayas. What would his dad have thought about his oldest son going so far from home to see the other side of the world? He would have been thrilled.

Linda gave her boys the best life she could. She swallowed her anger in a lot of situations, choked back her ebbing grief for their sake. Turning forty had been a drag, but what could she do? Linda still battled her weight, depression, and anxiety, and it never seemed to get any easier. One of the highlights of her day was getting up to watch *Body Electric,* an exercise show on PBS television hosted by Margaret Richard, a perky Tallahassee, Florida, woman who, much to Linda's delight, had a mantra of "Over 40 and fabulous." The routines were set to fun music, and sometimes Linda just sat back and watched the show to feel some sense of inspiration, even if it had to be used at a future date. Sometimes, she and her sister Debbie would talk about Margaret as if they knew her.

Linda watched what she ate, but the pounds didn't come off. In fact, she continued to gain. She tended to blame the meds, antidepressants and antianxiety pills. But Linda, based on her experience caring for her husband, knew otherwise. She knew she had to explore options and seek other opinions. So she went to see an endocrinologist at Millard Fillmore, a teaching hospital affiliated with the University of Buffalo. Sure enough, she was diagnosed with a thyroid disorder that caused lethargy, depression, and weight gain. Linda was relieved to find out that she had a glandular problem. "I knew it!" she exclaimed, laughing on the examination table as a few medical students looked on. "So it really isn't my fault that I'm fat—it's my glands!"

The doctor prescribed thyroid medication and right away, she began to feel better. The pounds came off, each loss heaven sent. Linda faithfully sweated to her favorite exercise program on PBS. Then something fairly unbelievable happened, something that would change Linda's life. The phone rang. It was her sister Debbie.

"You are never going to guess who just moved to Buffalo," Debbie queried.

"Who?" Linda asked. *Who the heck could she be talking about?*

"Margaret Richard."

It was true. The star of *Body Electric* had uprooted and landed in Buffalo. Debbie had confirmed it before phoning Linda. As it turned out, Margaret Richard had an even bigger fan—an Orchard Park lawyer named Jack Fox who started writing her letters saying he watched the show and was intrigued by her grace. They met and fell in love. Surely it had to be true love—Richard left Florida and moved to Buffalo. She'd started teaching exercise classes at a fitness center on Seneca Street, practically right in Linda's backyard. Linda started going to her classes three times a week. That one-hour workout session would become her refuge. And with a newly emboldened enthusiasm for fitness goals, Linda soon dropped thirty pounds. She had never felt better, physically. Everyone noticed and congratulated her on her new figure. It felt good, and she'd worked hard for it.

Donny would have been proud of her.

TO THE EXTENT she could logistically, Linda tried her best to keep Donny involved in family life. Graduation parties, christenings, birthdays, Fourth of July cookouts— the handicap van would shuttle him back and forth. Every year around Christmas, Linda and her brothers and sisters and aunts and uncles and numerous cousins held a special Mass in the back banquet room at the Irish Center. Donny almost always attended. Many of Linda's nieces and nephews had grown up being introduced to the "new

Donny," and so when it came to these parties, it was the young children who often were more than comfortable around him, sitting on his lap or asking how he was, more comfortable, say, than many of the adults, whose hearts understandably broke at the sight of Donny languishing in the land of the living dead. A lot of people, including the firemen who saved his life, wished at times that God had taken Donny back on that cold December morning.

In a way, the old Donny—the alive Donny, the thinking, feeling, loving, free-willed Donny—had died. Every doctor said the same thing: He was too far gone; he would never be the same. This was the best Donny that Linda and the boys could ever expect. One doctor once responded to Linda's question about Donny's possible recovery by simply saying: "Look at him." But Linda wasn't buying it. There had to be a way to fix him. She'd investigated light therapy, shock treatments, hyperbaric chambers. To a large extent she'd reached acceptance, but still felt that it was her duty to try everything she could, even if it led to only minimal improvement.

Toward the end of 2003 Linda arrived at Father Baker Manor for a monthly "care plan meeting," which involved Donny's social worker, Patricia Fernandes, and his chief clinical nurse, Lynn Hornberger, as well as a nutritionist and physical therapist. They sat together in a conference room briefing Linda and one another on what had been happening. In Donny's case, not much. He was undergoing physical therapy three days a week, but in terms of his veg-etative condition, there was no progress. Not even a grunt. There was talk of continued maintenance therapy to pre-vent atrophy, which Linda agreed was the right course, though there was no talk about how to fix a broken brain.

She left that meeting wondering about her next move. Perhaps alternative treatment. Taking him to a neurologist was out—that hand had been played, and every one of those doctors pretty much said the same thing: There was no real chance of recovery; there was nothing they could do.

Linda decided to take Donny to a special rehabilitation physician, a physiatrist. He had not been examined by such a specialist—traditionally called upon to help treat a range of conditions from severed spinal cords to separated shoul-ders—since his time at LEIR.

Although Linda hadn't been thrilled with the work of the last ECMC physiatrist with whom she had dealt, she nevertheless dialed the medical center and entered into a lengthy phone odyssey, navigating instructions from recorded messages, holding until she was transferred, hold-ing some more, each time having to explain from the beginning why she was calling. She was getting fed up but kept calm.

"Yes," Linda began yet again, biting her tongue, "my husband was a head-trauma patient there in '95 and '96 and I would like to have him examined by a physiatrist."

"Please hold while I transfer you."

Just when Linda was about ready to hang up, a woman on the other end of the phone informed her that, yes, there was a resident rehab physiatrist at ECMC who could see Donny. Linda accepted the first possible appointment, a few weeks before Christmas.

"What is the doctor's name?"

"You'll be seeing Dr. Jamil Ahmed."

Fourteen

IN THE SOUTHEAST CORNER of Pakistan, in the province of Sindh, along the banks of the River Indus, sits the tiny city of Shahdadpur. The city has its cultural charms, but the majority of its three hundred thousand or so inhabitants live in overcrowded, impoverished conditions. It is best known for the Punjabi legend that held that the mystical lovers Sohni and Mahinwal were washed up on the banks of the Indus next to each other, the symbol of eternal love.

As the story goes, Sohni, the most beautiful girl in all of Gujrat, a larger city upriver, was forbidden by her family to be with an unrefined former trader named Mahinwal. He was so distraught by the idea of a life without Sohni that he renounced all his possessions and lived outside the city as a hermit. So drawn to him, so touched by his love for her, Sohni used to sneak out at night and cross the river to see him, using a clay pot as a flotation device. One day, a chagrined sister-in-law found her pottery tucked away in the high grass near the river. To teach Sohni a lesson, the petty shrew switched it with a half-baked one. That night, the beautiful Sohni, trying to cross the Indus to be with her Mahinwal, sank. She was swept away by a strong current. Mahinwal heard her cry and tried to save her, but they both drowned. Their love, however, was unstoppable and inspired generations. The tomb of Sohni in Shahdadpur has forever been a draw for millions of Pakistani people from the Punjabi province, who to this day remain enchanted by the romantic folklore.

Shahdadpur is considered a rural relative to the larger cities, such as nearby Hyderabad, and in addition to tourism, is known for its textile and silk makers. It has businessmen and bankers and lawyers. Growing up the son of a prominent Shahdadpur attorney, Jamil Ahmed and his eight siblings attended the best schools in the city. One of his older brothers had become a judge, another a banker. Just as marriages are arranged in this part of the world, careers for young men are typically preset by parents. One day when he was fifteen, Jamil's father sat him down to discuss his options.

"You could be a lawyer or perhaps a banker like your brother," his father said. "Which do you think you might find more agreeable?"

Jamil, a shy kid with a good heart, thought for a moment. He wasn't sure he wanted to be either. "I want to help people," he told his father. "I'd like to be a doctor."

Eventually, Jamil did go to medical school, in the

capital city of Karachi, the biggest city in Pakistan. After his first year of studying medicine, Jamil returned to Shah-dadpur to visit his family. One of his first days back he noticed people kept coming by the house, asking to see him. Word had somehow spread that he was a doctor, and because there were so few medical practitioners available, many sick and injured people were desperate to pay him a visit. Although Jamil would patiently explain that in fact he was not yet a doctor but just in his first year at the Sindh Medical College, it didn't matter. Come on, said the hope-ful visitors, sometimes strangers, often relatives or friends of friends, couldn't he please just have a look? For some of the worst cases, Jamil agreed to at least take the sick per-son with him on the train back to Karachi, where he might help them find a doctor.

One day a young man came to Jamil's doorstep suffer-ing from a heart condition. A local physician had told him his heart valves were shot and that most likely he would die within weeks. There was nothing he could do. Surgery—expensive and complicated—would definitely kill him, the doctor had said. This way, he could take care of his affairs and live out his days with loved ones. He had been given up for dead. Jamil was home from school often—for political reasons, mainly government strikes, the college often shut down for months at a time. The young man at the door was breathing heavily, and in raspy, plaintive gasps begged for a second opinion. "They tell me I am going to die," the man said. "Please help me."

So Jamil Ahmed, unable to withstand the guilt of not doing anything, agreed to accompany the young man to Jinnah Hospital, the largest hospital in Karachi. Spending a long day standing on a crowded train and then later spending hours exploring the labyrinth that is the Pakistani health-care system, Jamil located a doctor willing to risk the heart valve surgery that would either kill the man or buy him a few extra months to a year. The operation was a success. When the man recovered, he was strong enough to undergo a second operation and then a third, until eventually his valves were restored to working order. He would owe his life to these procedures and the exceptionally kind medical student who was willing to help him even when it would have been easy to say "Sorry, but there's nothing I can do."

AND SO ON the December day in 2003 when Dr. Jamil Ahmed found himself in a narrow ECMC examination room face-to-face with Linda Herbert and her vegetative husband, he found himself empathizing. Linda had launched into a frustrated soliloquy while Dr. Ahmed stood by patiently listening.

"Everybody keeps telling me there is nothing we can do for him." Linda sighed. "I mean, yeah, I realize he's probably never going to wake up, I know that, but isn't there something we can try? Even to make him a little better? Even if it leads to just a little improvement, *anything?* I just want to try. I owe that to Don."

"Well, first of all," Dr. Ahmed explained when it was clear she was through and that he had the stage, "I don't like to tell people a patient such as your husband can never recover. I don't like to use the word *never,* because you know there is always some hope."

Dr. Ahmed was a slender man, in his early forties. Linda found his accent difficult to understand but liked what she was hearing. He glanced over some of Donny's old charts and asked Linda a few questions about his progress lately or lack thereof. Next to Linda sat Donny, in his wheelchair, head down, appearing asleep.

"Can he get up on the table?"

"No," Linda replied. "He doesn't move, not on his own. Maybe the thumbs-up, but that's pretty much it."

Dr. Ahmed unzipped Donny's coat and listened to his heartbeat. Normal. Then he whacked him on the knee with the physician's mallet to check reflexes. Donny's leg did not budge.

"Mr. Herbert!" Dr. Ahmed called out loudly. "Mr. Herbert, can you hear me? If you can hear me, look up!"

No response. Not even the remotest reflexive tracking of eyes to sound. The charts revealed Donny had pretty much made a round-trip, from a comatose to a minimally conscious state, to a brief, confusional conscious state, back to minimally conscious. Looking at him now, Dr. Ahmed had to guess Donny was more in line with the "close to persistent vegetative state" classification, but he didn't want to go downgrading him just yet.

"What I'm going to recommend is that we try different medications," Dr. Ahmed explained. "Different combinations of neurostimulants, low dosage, until we see any signs of change. I believe this is our best chance for some improvement."

"All right," Linda said. "Let's give it a try."

Thank you, Lord. Finally, someone willing to try.

"Thank you, Dr. Ahmed," Linda said. "It's been a long time since a doctor has given me any hope."

"Oh, you should never lose hope," Dr. Ahmed said with a pleasant smile. "May I ask, are you religious?"

"Excuse me?"

"Do you believe in God?"

"Yes, I do," Linda said. "I'm a Catholic. I've been praying for Donny every day."

"That's good."

A nonpracticing Muslim who since arriving in Buffalo had been to more Roman Catholic churches than mosques, Dr. Ahmed possessed a strong belief in God, or rather, the idea of a God, or some higher power that transcended any official religious affiliations or earthly definition. As both a resident rehab physician at Boston University

Medical Center and in the past few years at ECMC's Rehabilitation Medicine Department, he had seen many patients pull through the darkest of ordeals, the most critical conditions, and he felt in his heart that the reason wasn't always the medicine. Or maybe it was a combination of both—God helping those who helped themselves.

Regardless, Dr. Ahmed prescribed something that afternoon that took Linda by surprise.

He said: "If you believe in God, and you pray, God will help."

Fifteen

DRAWING FROM YEARS of experience with thousands of head injuries; a broad palette of approved pharmaceuticals, from attention deficit disorder drugs to Parkinson's disease pills; some updated academic research, as well as his own hunches about which chemical combinations might prompt Donny's brain into rebooting, Dr. Ahmed started the treatments. The meds would be delivered by the Father Baker nurses every morning with the rest of Donny's various PEG tube infusions. Dr. Ahmed instructed Linda to bring Donny back roughly every three months for an examination.

Dr. Ahmed was more or less flying blind; in fact, landing a plane with his eyes closed might have been easier than successfully rewiring a brain. Donny's PET scans showed widespread inactivity and atrophy. But at the same time, he was not dead. As evidenced by his mere physical existence, somewhere, deep in the brain stem, Donny's most primitive command centers were still open for business. His heart beat. His blood pumped. His lungs completed their life-giving tasks.

So what, then, was his brain? Ninety-eight percent dead? Seventy-five percent? Dr. Ahmed could not tell from a PET scan. Even the most gifted scientists with the most cutting-edge equipment could not have answered that question definitively. Looking to case studies, Dr. Ahmed found some precedent. There were a few remarkable examples from which to draw at least some hope—patients with traumatic brain injuries who'd come back from oblivion.

Just months earlier, in June 2003, a car-crash victim named Terry Wallis, in a shocker straight out of a Stephen King novel, emerged from a minimally conscious state after a staggering nineteen years. Over several days the Arkansas man, to the amazement and delight of his loved ones, regained the ability to communicate in mangled groans, convinced he was still nineteen and that Ronald Reagan was president. No one had ever before been in a comalike condition as long as Wallis and come back to regain the ability to speak.

Then there was the case of Gary Dockery, a Walden, Tennessee, policeman who in 1988 was propelled into the muted, motionless world of the minimally conscious after taking a bullet in the head. Seven-plus years later, Dockery stunned his family when he inexplicably began to speak for several hours, remembering his sons and camping trips. His speaking jag did not last long; Dockery died less than a year later.

In both of these cases, the patients had specific parts of

the brain traumatized by force. Furthermore, no one could explain *why* they had come back to close to normal.

But Donny's case was different. His entire brain had been grossly impaired, not just one or two sections. It was as if he suffered from Alzheimer's, autism, cerebral palsy, dementia, and a whole host of other degenerative mental disorders all at once. It was tough to find examples of anyone who had ever come back from such a serious injury, although just a few years earlier, right in Buffalo, Dr. Ahmed had treated a heart-attack victim who appeared to lose some brain function and fell into a comatose state while hooked up to a ventilator, only to wake up in the ICU smiling and talking a few days later. Eventually, he walked out of ECMC. But cases like these were extremely rare.

Dr. Ahmed's hope was that just the right combination of neurostimulants would spark Donny's brain into ignition, restore activity, produce signals, currents, and synapses where only emptiness and stupor had reigned. One of his earliest prescribed drug cocktails comprised one part Celexa, an antidepressant (40 milligrams) and a dash of Strattera, a drug commonly used to treat ADD. From the start, Donny didn't show much change, except some increased drooling and some sleep-cycle interruption. Dr. Ahmed later mixed and matched, working Sinemet, used commonly to treat Parkinson's, into the repertoire, as well as some cognitively friendly, metabolic activity–inducing vitamins like B-12 and folic acid.

Toward the end of 2004, more than a year into his experimental prescriptions, Dr. Ahmed was examining Donny and talking to Linda about slight signs of progress. One of the nurse's aides at Father Baker reported that Donny seemed to know he was being asked to move, seemed to go along with it.

Additionally, the terrible stiffness in Donny's muscle tone appeared to diminish. Less-rigid muscle tone meant more brain activity, as if an army of musculature system messengers had been stirred into a gathering assembly. But it was hard for Dr. Ahmed to know anything for sure. The chemicals intermingling in Donny's brain did their neuro-dance shrouded in a microscopic secrecy science might never be able to crack.

But Dr. Ahmed could observe the end product. And when he looked over at Donny, he noticed something else that was telling. A facial expression. Where once he had been a blank slate of catatonic bewilderment, Donny now seemed to exhibit something more humanistic. To the doctor, he looked a little depressed.

During yet another visit a few months later, Donny seemed to be crying. But Linda had seen Donny cry before at the nursing home. Dr. Ahmed took it as a positive sign. Maybe Donny *was* stirring around somewhere in there.

Sixteen

ANOTHER YEAR PASSED. Donny displayed no real improvement apart from some of the minor changes Dr. Ahmed had observed. Linda and the boys had resigned themselves to Donny's fate, having survived this long without him, though they never stopped hungering for the old Donny. As Linda had suspected from the start, having to stand by and watch Donny miss out on so many happy times was more difficult to bear as time passed, not less.

Linda had followed Donny's dream of going out west—with Patrick and Nicky. They took the ultimate outdoors vacation—Yellowstone, the Grand Tetons, and the Rocky Mountain National Park. Along the way, in a far more expansive wildlife sampling than found at Tifft Farm or the Erie Zoo, Linda and her two youngest boys saw condors with ten-foot wingspans, bald eagles, magnificent moose, and elk.

The true outdoorsman, though, was Patrick, who had interned with the United States Fish and Wildlife Service.

He had a genuine appreciation for nature. Patrick was also turning into quite the expert angler, much better than his dad, better than Donny ever could have imagined one of his kids would be. Patrick caught salmon in Lake Ontario, walleye in Lake Erie, and carp in the Buffalo River. All those years fishing with his boys, Donny may have only actually put his pole in the water but a few times. That's because he was too busy making sure that the boys had their hooks baited and reels properly set up, constantly untangling their lines with the patience of a saint. His patience had evidently paid off.

Patrick became Linda's go-to guy. He'd do anything for her. He was selfless, thoughtful, the middle child who became the superglue helping to keep the family dynamic together. As he grew taller, leaner, Patrick, most everyone agreed, was turning into the spitting image of Donny.

Tommy, meanwhile, was studying for the test to become a police officer down in Atlanta. He'd finished up at the University of Buffalo, and while he waited for a slot to open, he worked as a truck driver for a tanning-bed company. Every so often he checked with friends of his dad's to see if there was any word of an impending fire department test in Buffalo, but with the city in budget hell, there hadn't been a new BFD recruiting class in years.

Then there was Don junior, once again given to wander-lust. In mid-January of 2005 he'd set off on another adventure, back to the Far East—this time to Japan, Thailand,

and eastern India, where he was hoping to reach the foothills of the Himalayas and maybe even get a glimpse of Mount Everest. His backpacking coexplorer was a fellow anthropologist Don had gotten to know while working at Pan American Consultants, a commercial excavation company.

Nicky turned out to be the smartest of the bunch, and was a popular kid in South Buffalo. He cranked out a 90-plus average as a St. Agatha's seventh grader and skillfully brought computer literacy to Durant Street. Even Linda became proficient at e-mail, thanks to Nicky.

Linda remained in good shape physically and, all things considered, mentally, too. But sadly, *cruelly*, the same could not be said for yet another beloved man in her life, her father, Jack. The poor guy, months shy of seventy, was being overrun by dementia, the result of a mild stroke, and was slipping into his own haze, not unlike the one imprisoning Donny. It came on slightly at first, but grew noticeably worse around St. Patrick's Day 2002, after the sudden death of Jack's closest brother, Tom. A profound sadness, coupled with the amputation of his left leg, crushed Jack's spirit. Unwavering kindness and cheer were usurped by dour apathy and then, throughout 2003, a gradual fading. Jack was often idle in a recliner in the living room, a blanket over his head. The dementia continued to accelerate in 2004 to the point where Jack, after nearly fifty years of marriage, didn't even know he and Mary had been together that long.

When, Linda wondered, would she find herself visiting her husband *and* her father in nursing homes?

IT WAS DARK when the two travelers entered the city of Varanasi in northern India. Perched on the muddy Ganges River where the Varuna and Asi rivers converge, Varanasi, formerly known as Banaras and before that Kashi, was considered the most sacred place in all of India. One million Hindu pilgrims journeyed there each year, mainly to bathe in the Ganges, convinced that it could wash away their sins. Many others came simply to die, thousands of them, their cremation fires burning brightly. It is a Hindu's belief that the soul, if it exits the body in Varanasi, will bypass the hit-or-miss reincarnation stage and instead go directly to heaven.

As Don junior and his companion gazed out of the open-air windows of the packed, fetid train, an even stronger stench invaded their nostrils, a putrid mix of feces, sun-ripened garbage, incense, and, underpinning it all, something sulfuric: cremation fires. The travelers had spotted the white smoke in all directions as the train lurched into the station. Don Herbert Jr. gathered up his gear and yanked up his wrinkled, grimy jeans, which were literally falling off him. His only pair, these trusty denims were not only loose from constant wear and the frugal tourist's diet, but now also featured a huge, gaping tear along the backside, causing more than a few modest Hindus to call it to his attention. Tomorrow, he knew, he would have to do an emergency repair.

Averse to trekking around any strange city at night, let alone trying to traverse these ancient, serpentine alleyways with his pants falling off him, Don junior made a suggestion to his friend Wade. "It's late. I say we walk to the nearest hotel. We'll have a look around tomorrow when it's light out."

Wade couldn't argue. They set off to find the cheap hostel they'd circled in their guidebook, secured a night's lodging, and tried to get some rest.

BY THE SPRING OF 2005, Father Baker Manor had obtained state permission to expand its short-term physical rehabilitation offerings. A rotating cast of care recipients was a boost to the bottom line, so a transitional reorganization was put in motion. The rooms on Sterling Court wing, closer to the rehab center, were earmarked for short-term residents, while the Opal wing would be solely for long-term residents, such as Donny Herbert. In mid-March he was moved.

There was something curious about Opal, something not a lot of people discussed. On two separate occasions, nurses there had noted strange, eerily similar happenings on the wing. Two elderly women, having never met, reported seeing a peaceful man in a black cloak and a black hat pass by their rooms at night and look in on them. In both cases, the women were compelled to ask aloud, "Who was that man in the black hat?" To which attending staffers would reply with a shrug, "There was no man in a black hat." And in both cases, one of the Opal residents died during the night.

The stories were perceived as odd, mildly freaky, more conversation pieces than paranormal phenomena. But a few of the nurses did talk about it, sometimes late at night, and they had a theory as to who the man in black garb might be. The black cloak, perhaps priestly vestments; the hat, an old monsignor's cap.

LINDA HAD HER HANDS full overseeing the planning and arranging of her parents' fiftieth anniversary party. With her father's health slipping away and her mom lobbying for a low-key celebration, the challenge was to put together something special without going overboard. The banquet hall in the back of the Irish Center seemed to be a perfect spot, because it was close and it would be easy for her dad to get in and out.

Jack and Mary's actual anniversary fell on Saturday, April 30, but since the hall wasn't available that day, Linda reserved it for the preceding Friday night, the twenty-ninth. Along with her sister Debbie, Linda spent hours crafting a special invitation and getting a list of family and friends who still lived in the area. In a delightful touch, some of Mary's distant cousins, a group of sisters scattered around New England, would reunite in Buffalo for the event. The old homestead at 77 Spaulding became the official party-planning headquarters. Mary made soup and sandwiches and kept the coffee percolator filled as the two sisters dug out phone numbers, licked envelopes, and mined dozens of old family photo albums.

For weeks that spring, Linda and Debbie were at their parents' home, taking care of details. Whenever they would talk about the party, Jack would say, "What party? What anniversary?" And when Linda and Debbie would say, "Your fiftieth," Jack would insist he hadn't been married that long. It was a bittersweet time, a final curtain drawing closed, one last chance to meaningfully reconnect before their dad's mind dissolved away completely. Jack literally could not recall his morning meal even as the toast crumbs collected on the front of his gray Bills sweatshirt. He'd sit at the kitchen table in his wheelchair eating everything in sight because he had forgotten that he'd just eaten. He stopped putting on his artificial leg, since the stump was always swollen and irritated. He became increasingly somber, withdrawn. This was a very painful time for Mary.

The day of the party, Linda squared away the menu and paid the caterers, and Debbie ordered a special cake from Pumpernick N' Pastry in Kaisertown. Several of

Linda's other siblings went over early that afternoon and decorated the hall, laying tablecloths and later adding centerpieces of floating candles. The room looked nice.

That night, Linda had a tough choice. She knew Donny would have wanted to be there, but realistically, it was too much for her with everything else going on. He would have to miss the party. Around seven P.M., Linda, Nicky, Tommy, and Patrick shuffled into the Irish Center. Don junior was somewhere in India. Donny was fast asleep at Father Baker Manor.

WHEN LINDA SAW her parents, her brothers and sisters, the grandchildren and relatives, she was overwhelmed. Somehow, fantastically, the party had all come together, a fitting tribute to Jack and Mary. They had struggled for a half century to provide for eleven children. This was the least they deserved.

An atmosphere of good cheer was accompanied by the soothing din of pleasant conversation. While cake and coffee were being served, Linda started the video presentation. Nicky's photo montage would be the highlight of the party. Linda and Debbie had picked out the pictures; Debbie's husband, Steve Corbett, scanned them onto a disk. But Nicky put it all together and added the music, songs such as the Beatles' "In My Life" and Kenny Rogers's "Through the Years." It started with vintage shots of Jack and Mary, just kids, on their wedding day in 1955, then slowly, chronologically, photographs of all their kids came in rapid succession, just as the babies had come in real life, from firstborn, John, to the seven daughters, Sharon, Peggy, Teresa, Linda, Debbie, Mary, and Jean, and the second oldest boy, Patrick, who'd become a fireman, and of course the two youngest, the bookends, Michael and David.

Some of the photos of Christmas morning on Spaulding were indeed a sight to behold, as everyone realized just how many presents Jack and Mary made sure were under that tree, not just a few per kid, but entire piles for each of the children. They must have saved all year to pull that off.

Family members delighted in seeing how everyone had grown and changed over the years. At one point a photo appeared of Donny and Linda on their wedding day in January of 1981, a beaming pair of inseparable nineteen-year-olds. In that split-second, Linda couldn't help but think about how her twenty-fifth wedding anniversary was approaching, how much fun it would be if her kids were planning a big party for them. Since the accident, Donny and Linda's wedding anniversary for the most part went unacknowledged by the family. But it always remained a special day for Linda.

Another photo of Linda and Donny appeared. In this one the two of them were dancing at a party held a decade earlier for Jack and Mary's fortieth wedding anniversary. It had been taken just a few months before Donny's accident. Here was Donny, the way everyone remembered him last—handsome, smiling, glowing with life, his old happy self. Like the other photos, the image only appeared for a second or two, but it somehow seemed longer, and as it lingered it brought a hallowed stillness to the room. Everyone, in their own way, at that precise moment, wished only good for Donny. The love for him could be felt from one end of the hall to the other. Mary whispered a quick prayer for Donny's recovery, as did Aunt Ellen and several others in the room.

Linda's sister Teresa experienced the weirdest vibe, a hair-raising flutter along her neck and shoulders, as yet another photo from Nicky's montage flashed on the big screen. This one was of Grandma Yvonne Terzian, Mary's mother. She'd passed away two years earlier. At that very instant, it felt to Teresa as if her grandmother were right there in the room with them. In the photograph, Yvonne, a tough-as-nails, deeply spiritual French Canadian woman who had been raised in an orphanage, bore a bountifully cheerful smile, as if ready to burst. Teresa felt something strange was happening, or about to happen. Yvonne had adored Donny, appreciated his willingness to always help her, fixing a broken washing machine, shoveling her driveway, and through the years she never stopped praying for him. Before she died, Yvonne promised Linda that when she got to heaven she was going to put in a good word for Donny.

Teresa, who had always been a little psychic, could

feel her heart racing. She was sure she was hearing from her grandmother. Yvonne seemed to be telling Teresa, not aloud, not in these exact words, not in words at all, but rather by way of this fleeting, funny feeling Teresa was experiencing, something to this effect: *Wait until you see the anniversary present that I have in store.*

Seventeen

THE NEXT DAY, Linda slept until ten A.M. The party had been a huge success, but she was exhausted. On the agenda for the day was shopping for a new rug. Her mission would take her to the suburb of Cheektowaga, near the Galleria Mall. This should have been a fairly simple mission, but in Linda's experience, so little in life turned out that way.

Linda knew exactly what she was looking for: a sizable, shaggy, kind of cool but not too expensive area rug for a sunroom addition she was having installed on Durant, along with a new rear deck. A new wooden floor had been freshly laid, and the entire project was nearly complete. Contractors had worked all winter on the additions to the home. Linda embarked on the project specifically so that when Donny came to visit from the nursing home in the warmer months, he could sit out back in his wheelchair and feel the sun on his face without neighbors or passersby gawking at him.

Linda fixed some breakfast, thanked Nicky for doing

such a good job on the video, and was on the road by eleven A.M. Some coupons led her to Linens 'n Things on this mild spring morning, but every rug in the store seemed either too plain or, alternatively, too dainty. She would have to try somewhere else.

AT AROUND TWO P.M. Donny Herbert was seated in his wheelchair by a window in a common lounge area near the nurses' station in the Opal wing of Father Baker Manor. A wall-mounted television set played softly above him. All of a sudden he shook his legs like an uncomfortable sleeper thrashing around in a bad dream.

Not far away, Jessica Mann, a twenty-two-year-old certified nursing assistant, milled about the station desk chatting with colleagues, trying to kill the last hour of her shift before her relief came on. She'd been on duty since seven A.M. and was tired. She thought she heard Donny Herbert say something, but of course that couldn't be since no one had ever heard him say anything before. She went over to him. She could not believe her ears.

Donny was talking.

His first real words in nearly nine years, and which he kept repeating in a sort of a slurred growl, were: "Where's Linda?"

DESPITE AN HOUR rifling through every rug in stock, Linda couldn't seem to find the particular one she had envisioned. Her mission was shaping up to be a bust, but one of the assistant managers suggested she try another location. Driving farther north on the thruway to a sister outlet in Williamsville, Linda had no reason to think the selection there would be any less old-ladyish, but she took a shot. After another fairly exhaustive search, she finally found what she had been searching for: a thick shag rug, with a bold black-and-white checkerboard pattern.

The morning had been a success after all. As she loaded her quarry into the back of her Explorer, Linda checked her cell phone and noticed that she'd missed two calls. One was from the nursing home, one from her home.

She called home first. Her youngest, Nick, answered. He'd been tooling around on Google Earth.

"The nurse at Father Baker just called. She wants you to call her," he told his mom. "I gave them your cell phone number."

"Okay," Linda replied. "Yeah, they called me. I'm going to call them right now. See you in a little while."

Linda hung up and quickly rang the main number of Father Baker, and then asked to be transferred to the nurses' station in the Opal wing. She waited in the half-filled parking lot, which was totally silent except for the faint sounds of the wind and the traffic whipping down Transit Road. On her cell phone, a nurse's aide named Jessica was carrying on about something that made no sense.

Donny had asked for her. Linda figured the nurses were experimenting with some alternative form of voice-stimulation therapy as part of Father Baker's new era of advanced rehab. So she went along with it. Then Jessica said she was going to hand the phone to Donny.

"Okay," Linda said, fumbling to get her car keys out of her purse. "Hi, Don, it's me, Linda," she said loudly.

"Lin, where are you? Come get me."

Linda froze. *What the . . . ?*

"Don, where are *you?*"

Linda, of course, knew exactly where he was; she'd just called there. But she instinctively tried to evaluate Donny's mental state. Surely, he was dazed. Perhaps in some trance? But it was Donny speaking for sure.

"I'm at One Eighty-two Melrose," he replied, clear as could be. *His childhood home.*

"Okay, I'm coming," Linda said. "Put Jessica on the phone."

She did not want to upset him. Linda could hear Donny call out, "Jessica!" and then mutter to himself, "Jessica, who's Jessica?"

"Listen, I'm on my way," Linda told the nurse's aide. *Could it be?* She started up the Explorer in a state of shock and darted out of the parking lot onto Transit Road, heading toward the thruway. The drive home would take at least twenty-five minutes—she had to grab Nick—and then it was another twenty minutes to get to the nursing home on Powers Road in Orchard Park. Linda's body seemed to surge with adrenaline as she drove.

Will he even still be talking when I get there? Does this mean he might get better? I've got to tell the kids!

Linda got her youngest back on the phone and delivered explicit orders. If Donny really was back from his zombielike stupor, she had to do everything she could to keep him coherent.

"Nick, listen to me, I want you to call the nursing home!"

"What's going on?"

"Your father is talking."

"What?"

"He's talking! I spoke with him just now! Now, listen to me, I want you to call the nursing home and have them put you on the phone with him—do you understand me? Keep him talking until I get there. I'll come pick you up as fast as I can."

"What should I say to him?" Nick asked.

"You guys both love to fish," Linda fired back. "Talk to him about fishing."

Linda hung up and next dialed her mother, Mary, who was just then putting on a percolator of coffee in the old kitchen at 77 Spaulding. She had been unwrapping some final golden jubilee gifts as she said good-bye to her cousins who'd flown in from New Hampshire. Teresa had just stopped by. She still had not told anyone about her strange sensation the night before.

Meanwhile, not more than a hundred yards down Durant Street, Nicky Herbert was about to have a real conversation with his father for the very first time.

Eighteen

H
I, DAD, it's me, Nick."
The boy paused in the tranquillity of the kitchen for what might come next, his throat tightening, his heart pounding. Just a day earlier, while putting the finishing touches on the anniversary video, Nick had stared at the old photographs of his father and imagined for a moment what his dad might have been like—before. He always wondered. Now he could find out.

Back at the nursing home, Donny was confused, growing agitated. Jessica did her best to calm him as staff members, especially ones who'd been working on Sterling Court, came running over to see and hear for themselves what was happening.

"This can't be Nicholas," Donny said.

Nick sat there, still trying to think of something to say. Donny had called out to Jessica, "This isn't Nicholas—he's just a baby, he can't talk!

"Are any of the other boys around? Is Donny there? Tommy, or Patrick? Who *is this?*"

Nicky was speechless. Words literally failed to form. His jaw was immobile. In that blink of a moment, he absorbed the sound of his father's voice like a heavy blow to the body. Then he finally replied, "Tommy and Patrick aren't here."

This wasn't exactly true. Tommy was crashed out in his room. Patrick was home for the weekend from Brockport State, but at the moment was over at his girlfriend Carrie's house.

Nicky continued. "It's me, Nick. Why do you think it's not me?"

"Because Nicky can't talk. Put one of the other boys on."

Nicky kept his composure. "I can talk," he said. "Do you know how old I am?"

"No, how old are you?"

"I'm thirteen."

"Holy shit."

Nicky chuckled and tried to change the subject.

The stop-and-start chitchat stalled. Nicky reached for words that did not come. After all these years of yearning to speak to his father, Nick could not think of a single thing to say. He struggled for a topic. But right then he remembered what his mother had told him earlier.

"So, do you like fishing?"

"Sure," his dad replied. "Love it."

"What kind of fish do you like to catch?"

"I don't know, anything . . . trout . . . bass."

And just like that, Nick and his dad began talking

to each other, easily, for the first time in their lives. They talked about fishing for walleye in the Buffalo River, and down at the Erie Basin Marina. Then Nick told him how Patrick had become a skilled bow hunter. Their conversation lasted no more than a few minutes, but, oddly, Donny seemed to somehow accept that perhaps it really was his toddler son with whom he'd been conversing.

"Mom will be here any minute, and then we're coming to see you," Nick told his dad. "So I'm going to hang up now. We'll be there soon, okay?"

"Okay," Donny said with a calm wheeze. "I'll see you in a little while."

"Sure thing, Dad," Nick said. "I love you."

Moments earlier Donny Herbert was not even certain with whom he'd been conversing. Yet the words came, words that Nick had always wanted to hear.

"I love you, too."

WHEN THE LAST of the anniversary presents—stained glass, books, a picture frame—had been opened over cake and coffee on Spaulding, Mary offered thanks and kisses and began to collect the crumpled wrapping paper, signaling that the celebration, so lovingly begun the night before, was officially over. Her cousins said their good-byes and readied themselves for their trip back to New England.

"Well, that's it," Mary said.

Just then, as if on cosmic cue, the wall phone in the kitchen rang. Teresa felt a sudden chill.

There was still one more present.

Mary answered and right away it was clear by her "My God!" and from the expression on her face that she had received startling news. She hung up the phone and turned to her daughter.

"What happened?" Teresa asked.

"That was Linda." Mary replied with a sniffle, her heart filling up with joy and her beautiful smiling eyes welling with tears. "I think we just got the best anniversary gift ever."

Nineteen

OUTSIDE THE WINDOW in the Opal wing of Father Baker Manor was a small patch of green with a gazebo in the center. Spring was in the air. Maple trees were budding. The sky was a mixture of wispy clouds and glints of sunshine.

These were sights that a once-avid outdoorsman like Donny would have appreciated more than most. But because of his cortical blindness, a condition in which his otherwise undamaged eyes were rendered useless because of his brain trauma, Donny could not see. His sense of vision may have been the result of his pupils responding to light, or an outright hallucination. But Donny was convinced he could see. Strangely, he knew, or rather, he appeared to know, that a window was there to be gazed through.

"Where is my wife?" Donny asked. "She said she was coming to get me."

"She's coming," Jessica said. "She'll be here soon."

Donny could not accept that the voice on the phone

had been little Nicky. He became increasingly distraught. Jessica wheeled him back to his room. Where was he? Where were Linda and the boys?

PATRICK HERBERT WAS first to arrive. He'd been a mere ten minutes away.

Any other twenty-year-old SUNY Brockport student might have been standing around a keg on a Saturday afternoon in the last throes of spring semester, but the quiet environmental science major preferred lures to liquor. When not in class or researching his thesis on restoring the walleye population in Lake Erie, Patrick fished, from the Finger Lakes to Caz Crick. Recently, as part of his research, he had navigated the Buffalo River in a SUNY Brockport fishing vessel, methodically stunning samples of walleye, tagging them, then releasing them back into the water in an effort to track their numbers in the months ahead. Almost every single weekend he made the one-hour drive back to Buffalo for his research and to visit his family, but mostly to spend time with his girlfriend, Carrie Lynch. She was a short, cute girl who lived with her parents in Orchard Park. Patrick and Carrie had started dating as high school seniors, around the time he had begun to break out of his shell. But it was Carrie, who attended the all-girls Mount Mercy Academy down the street from Timon, who had to ask him to her prom.

Because Carrie lived near Father Baker Manor, the two

of them would often visit Donny together. Unlike his older brothers, Patrick did not find the visits too painful. He would sit for two hours or more and shoot the breeze, telling his father about his life, about school, about Carrie, about hunting and fishing. Donny may have been mute and lifeless, but Patrick was still content to ramble on. Carrie found it sad to watch, but knew that these sessions were meaningful. In some unknown way, she felt Donny must have appreciated them, too.

As Patrick sat in Carrie's living room watching the Discovery Channel, her cell phone rang.

"It's your mom," she told him, glancing at the caller ID.

No big deal, Patty thought. He didn't own a cell phone. His mother probably needed him to give Nicky a ride somewhere. But Carrie found it strange that her boyfriend's mother was calling on her phone. Linda had never called her before.

"Quick," Linda told Carrie, "you guys have to get to the nursing home. Patrick's dad is talking!"

Though Linda's tone conveyed urgency, Carrie for some reason didn't give it much import. She assumed that Linda meant Donny had been trying to vocalize, and she found it touching that Linda should think this urgent enough to call to Patrick's attention. When Carrie relayed the message, Patrick likewise assumed his dad must be having a good day, or a *better than normal* day. Possibly, he was giving a feeble thumbs-up signal or making garbled noises in response to yes or no questions.

But Patrick was more than willing to immediately drop what he was doing and drive right over to Father Baker's. Not because he was bursting with excitement. He had no idea what was going on. No, if he made a decision to rush over it was for no other reason than because his mother had asked him to.

A few moments later, as he lingered outside by his truck, Carrie still getting ready, Patrick began to think about his mother's message, almost daydreaming.

What if his dad really was talking?

Patrick grew impatient as he waited for Carrie to find a certain pair of sneakers in a closet full of equally adequate footwear. Normally laid-back, he suggested they take two cars, that she should just meet him at the nursing home, but Carrie convinced him to wait just a little longer.

When they arrived at his father's room, Donny was inside, alone, facing the open doorway. His quarters were tight but clean, the size of an ordinary hospital room, with a bathroom to the left of the door and a heavy-duty, metal-railed bed. Some family photos hung on a bulletin board, along with a cluster of get-well notes and holy cards.

Normally, Donny would be slumped in his wheelchair, head hung low, eyes glazed over. But now he was sitting straight, head upright, eyes wide open. He appeared attentive, as if expecting someone. He looked in the direction of his son.

Right away Patrick was overcome by a positive feeling. To be greeted by such a scene was unlike anything he'd ever witnessed in all these years of coming to visit. His dad seemed *there*.

As he walked through the doorway, Carrie followed behind in nervous disbelief. Then Patrick blurted out at the top of his voice, "Hey, Dad, it's me!"

Donny Herbert looked directly at his son, and in an excited voice gasped, "Wow . . . *Patty.*"

The twenty-year-old almost fell down. He turned to Carrie, who looked dazed. Donny's words, loud, clear, intense, knocked them both back like thunderclaps. Neither could fathom what their ears had just absorbed. But they had heard it; they had heard Donny speak.

Tears filled both their eyes. Patrick moved in a little closer.

"Hey, Dad, can I have a hug?"

Without hesitation, Donny Herbert smiled and opened his arms.

"IT'S TRUE," Carrie excitedly told Linda. "He's back."

Carrie was outside in the hallway of the nursing home talking on her cell phone. Inside Donny's room, crying, shell-shocked, Patrick leaned against the wall across from the bed, unsure—perhaps for the first time—of what to say. His father, wearing a navy blue BFD T-shirt and gray sweatpants, sat a few feet away from him in his wheelchair near the door. He seemed at peace. His customary grimace was replaced now by a far more serene expression, as if freed from some unholy possession.

Carrie did her best to brief Linda on their extraordinary encounter.

"Is he confused or upset?" Linda inquired breathlessly, still tearing down I-90 west. "Does he know what happened to him?"

"He seems pretty calm," Carrie said. "Patrick is talking to him."

"Oh, my gosh," Linda interjected. "What did they say to each other?"

Not remotely knowing where or how to begin, Patrick, as it turned out, had started by formally, alas finally, introducing Carrie to his dad. Donny, in turn, could not believe that a little ten-year-old squirt like Patrick had a girlfriend. Patrick didn't correct him, not yet. Linda didn't know whether to laugh or cry as Carrie recalled the conversation.

"What else did he say?" she asked.

Choking up, Carrie provided an answer: "He asked for you, Mrs. Herbert."

Linda's heart burst with joy.

"He keeps asking for you."

TOMMY HERBERT FINALLY got up from his bed and shuffled downstairs. Thirsty, groggy from a late night, the twenty-three-year-old could barely comprehend what Nick was saying. "What do you mean you talked to Dad?"

Nick played it cool. "I talked to him just now, on the phone."

Tommy looked at him like he had just gone insane, but Nick, his tone plain, straightforward, began to tell his brother some of the details of their conversation.

Tommy stood in the kitchen, more skeptical than dumbfounded, but taking it all in.

Nicky wouldn't make this up—would he?

The home on Durant Street grew quiet. In those last few moments before Linda arrived to retrieve them, Nicky sat back down at the computer, his mind replaying everything his father had said. *He liked hunting with the bow better than a gun.*

Tommy went back up to his room, his body coursing with nervous energy.

Just then Tommy received a call from his girlfriend of five years, Caitlin Fitzpatrick. Caitlin had just finished her shift at J. Crew in the Galleria Mall and was on her way to South Buffalo. She wanted to remind Tommy that they had a late-afternoon family event to attend, a retirement supper for her mother. She was on her way over. Perhaps he should think about getting ready?

"Well, we have to go to the nursing home," Tommy intoned.

Beneath Tommy's hard edge was a gentle, good-natured guy. Even hungover, the idea of having to spiff up for an early-bird retirement dinner probably wouldn't have bothered him all that much. But Caitlin could sense the tension in his voice. Moreover, in all their years together, Caitlin could count on two hands the number of times he had visited his father at the nursing home. Something must be wrong, she thought.

"Why, Tommy, what is it?"

"My dad is talking."

Zipping through the mall's employee parking lot, Caitlin slammed on the brakes and shouted, "What do you mean—what's going on?!" Her voice was overcome with the unbridled hope with which Tommy should have been bursting. But if Caitlin was ecstatic, Tommy kept his guard up.

"Stop," Tommy barked, cutting off her gleefully curious interrogation. "Please stop. We don't know what's happening yet. This could be nothing."

"Okay, okay." Caitlin sighed as she drove on, her hands trembling the whole way. When she got to the Herberts' home on Durant, Nicky was in the kitchen, still waiting for his mother, now only five minutes away. Caitlin, elated, ran inside and hugged her boyfriend. But Tommy remained stone-faced, gently pushing her aside.

"Please," Tommy said. "Just stop."

Caitlin understood why he was being so cold and let it go. She wanted to ask Tommy for more information, but she kept to herself, as if it were any normal day.

After a few tense minutes, Tommy admitted to what Caitlin already knew.

"I don't want to get my hopes up," he said.

A HORN HONKED in the driveway. Linda had arrived. Nick hopped in. Tommy and Caitlin followed in her car.

"Did you talk to Dad?" Linda asked Nicky as she pulled out onto South Park Avenue.

"Yeah," Nick answered, still in shock but ready for whatever might come next.

"How did he sound?" she pressed. "Good, right? Just a little different?"

"I don't know," Nicky replied matter-of-factly. "I can't remember ever hearing him speak before."

Right at that moment, Linda's heart broke all over again as the reality of just how much had been lost engulfed her. They drove in silence. Nick thought back to an old memory, possibly his earliest.

He did remember the sound of his father's voice. "Stay back," he'd said.

What will I say when I get there? Nick thought. *How long will he keep talking?*

As they pulled up to the nursing home, Nicky took a deep breath. Linda was excited, nervous, but remarkably poised. Tommy and Caitlin pulled right up beside them, and the four of them entered the facility together.

Patrick was there to greet them. Tommy looked at his brother. *It's real,* Patrick's teary eyes told him.

Carrie was crying. Caitlin, too, began to weep. Linda, wearing a navy South Buffalo sweatshirt and a pair of black sweats, entered the room, her heart in her throat.

"Don?"

"*Lin!*"

Linda spun back around now to register what had just come out of Donny's mouth. Looking back at her three boys, who were now crowded near the doorway, all of them crying as the magnitude of this turn of events took hold of them, Linda was flush with emotion—excitement, shock, joy. She ran toward Donny, the husband she'd lost nearly ten years ago. She hugged him for what seemed like a thousand times at once.

Nick and Patrick were smiling, hugging each other. Tommy was stunned, his jaw slack. "I don't think I can go to dinner with your family tonight," he told Caitlin in a monotone.

In that small room at Father Baker Manor, around three P.M., the Herbert family drew together in an almost tribal embrace. Tears of joy streamed down their cheeks, as nursing home staffers crowded outside the door. But one important family member was missing: Don junior, who was off in some remote corner of the globe.

Later that night, Linda would send her son an e-mail, uncertain when, if ever, he might receive it. Her opening line: "Donny, I don't know how to tell you. But I think we experienced a true miracle today."

Twenty

TERESA PULLED OUT the loosely stapled Xerox sheets with the names and phone numbers of everyone in her family and went straight down the list. She wanted to move fast so she herself could get to the nursing home. She was excited to be the bearer of such good news. But right away something dawned on her that she hadn't anticipated: No one believed her.

The reason, beyond the staggering improbability of her report, was this: Teresa had a well-documented history of playing April Fool's jokes while growing up. She'd pulled every leg in her family at some point over the years. Although it was a half day away from the first of May, her siblings assumed she was invoking some rarely used grace period—or something—because Donny could not possibly be talking. "Isn't it a little late for April Fool's jokes?" asked her sisters, one after the other. But Teresa just repeated as fast as she could, "Don's talking; get to the nursing home," and moved on down the list.

Her brother Pat, a fireman, was downright furious. "Teresa, don't fuck with me like this!"

"Listen, Pat, it's true. It's a miracle. Just get out to the nursing home!"

That's basically how it went. Everyone, at least at first, thought Teresa was a hoaxer, with questionable decorum, at that. There was, of course, one person who believed her right away: good old Aunt Ellen. Ellen and her husband, Jim, lived in Orchard Park, near Father Baker Manor, and they rushed right over. Sensing that Linda and the boys needed some privacy, Aunt Ellen decided she would make herself useful.

"We have to tell Simon!" Ellen shouted to her husband.

Uncle Simon had always been a father figure to Donny. Ellen called Simon's cell phone, but Simon wasn't answering. Ellen must have dialed it five times in a row. "Come on, Jim, let's go," she said. "We have to find Simon."

Jim drove her over to Simon and Kathy's house only a few hundred yards away from the nursing home. Pounding on the front door and shouting at the top of her lungs, Ellen ended up scaring one of Simon's young nephews. The startled teenager, in turn, hurriedly dialed Simon's cell phone. Seeing the call coming from his house this time, Simon picked up.

"Uncle Simon, there's some crazy lady knocking on the door!"

Simon was driving on the thruway on his way to the

mall. He pulled off to the shoulder of the road and listened to the messages from Ellen, whom he assumed to be buzzed or just plain daffy. But then again, she'd gone to his house, and here she was *calling on his cell again.*

Simon answered this time and when he heard what Ellen was saying, that Donny had asked for Linda and that she and the boys had rushed over to be with him, he went pale. "You want to repeat that one more time?"

"Don's talking."

"Holy . . ."

Aunt Ellen had owed Donny a favor.

BY FOUR O'CLOCK, Donny's room was filling up: Linda, the three boys, the girlfriends, Carrie and Caitlin, Aunt Ellen, and Teresa, not to mention aides and orderlies from all sides of the nursing home. Linda kept asking the nurses whether a doctor could be summoned, but neither Dr. Eileen Reilly, who was the primary visiting physician for the Opal wing, nor Dr. Ahmed, could be located.

Everyone was walking on eggshells. No one wanted to upset Donny. He figured out that he'd been out cold for a spell, but he didn't know yet for how long. "A long time, Don," was all Linda could bear to tell him. No matter what any of the kids relayed—that George Bush's son was now the president, that Tommy was going to be a police officer—Donny would scoff.

What Donny wanted to know was *how long?* Three months? He clung to the idea that that's all it had been.

Linda placed a white towel over Donny's chest, an oversized bib. He kept closing and opening his eyes, which seemed irritated by the brightly illuminated room. He appeared to be trying to focus, however impossible. His face, gaunt but still handsome, was an ever-shifting portrait of expressions, from delight to despair to confusion. But the more he heard, the more he took in—Nicky was in seventh grade, Patrick drove a Toyota—the more distressed he became.

"How long have I been out?"

He wept. No one knew what to say in that difficult moment. Just then, broad-shouldered Simon Manka, in a bright red T-shirt and a pair of jeans, walked into the room, having gotten there as quickly as he could. Linda stood by the side of Donny's wheelchair, trying to reassure him while controlling the pace and the amount of information coming at him, whispering directives, identifying voices. She was Donny's trusted guide for the overwhelming events that hit him with a fury.

"Don, somebody is here to see you," Linda told him. "See if you recognize his voice."

Simon stretched out his big paw and let it come to rest on Donny's shoulder. "Well, you can't be half as upset as I am about being old."

Right away Donny recognized the hearty voice. "Simon!"

The room exploded with cries and laughter and hand claps as Simon gave Donny a big hug. It was a scene no one would soon forget.

Simon whispered Donny a heartfelt "How ya doin', buddy," as the two embraced.

Donny smiled but remained anxious. Then he began to cry again. Something was not right. Sobbing uncontrollably, he asked Simon, "How long have I been gone?"

Linda's eyes told Simon it was his call.

"Quite a while, pal," Simon said, while fighting tears and patting Donny gently on the shoulder. "Quite a while."

"How long?"

"Ten . . . ten years."

Donny, so durable to have finally come back after all that time, absorbed the blow with a tormented gasp. Beside himself, his eyes clenched shut as he continued to sob, Donny reached out for Linda.

"We've been here for you the whole time," she said.

"How old am I?"

"Forty-three," Linda said.

"Oh, my god," Donny said. He was smiling through his tears now.

Shouted Simon, "I'm fifty-two, man!"

No one knew what to say next as they watched Donny struggling to make sense of this, his eyes getting saucery, his forehead tightening, as a no-holds-barred wrestling match raged in his mind. His hair was tousled in competing directions from all the boys touching and hugging him. Donny was reeling. Linda took her husband by the hand.

"You kept your muscles strong. You had a good attitude. You did your rehab. You did it, Don, you came back to us."

Donny, through a mouthful of spittle, mumbled halfheartedly, "Well, I must have done something."

"You sure did, pal," Simon said.

"You never gave up, Don," Linda added. "You *never* gave up."

Twenty-one

EVERYONE TOOK TURNS talking with Donny. Now it was Linda's younger brother, Pat, who knelt down before the wheelchair, as if living out a waking dream. A thirty-four-year-old fireman, he was sure glad he'd raced out to see this. Teresa hadn't been screwing around after all. Donny was back, and Pat had never felt more thrilled about anything since the birth of his son, Matthew, six months before Donny's accident.

There was a bond that linked Pat and Donny, one that took hold that terrible year. Donny, after all, was Matthew's godfather, penciled in at St. Agatha's at the last minute, a special godparent for a special child, even if he couldn't be there for him.

Not long after the accident, Pat received another blow: His son Matthew was diagnosed as being severely autistic. In the years that followed, Pat found out the meaning of *severe*. His marriage ended and he took on the struggle of single-handedly raising the handicapped child. As Matthew grew older, it was apparent that he was far worse off than even the doctors had predicted. Matt could not speak. He had virtually no control of his faculties. He was helpless. Donny's kindred spirit.

"All the guys in the department ask about you, Donny, all the time," Pat said, taking his turn. "Gary O'Neill, Paddy Coghlan, you remember him, don't you? He was your lieutenant."

Donny smiled, then his face relaxed. Easy one. Of course he knew Coghlan.

Pat smiled, too.

"Oh, and I've got good news for you, Donny—you quit smoking."

Everyone in the room laughed.

"This is a great day, Donny," Pat said. "A great day."

Twenty-two

THEIR BASEBALL CAPS pulled snug, just like kids again, Tommy and Patrick took turns talking to their dad. Nick shot some video with a digital camera one of the male nurses had retrieved from his car. But Donny kept reaching out and asking for Linda. She handed him a photo of all four boys taken recently in front of the house on Durant. Donny fumbled with it angrily, staring for a second as if he could see, not knowing he was looking at the back of the photo. He dropped it. "I can feel it, I just can't see it!"

Linda turned it over and tried moving it farther away.

"It's a blur," Donny said. "I'm lost. I can hear you, but I can't see you."

"We're going to take care of you, Don," Linda said. "Don't worry."

Donny leaned his head back and muttered, "Geez . . . this is a lot."

He began to cry again, all the while repeating, "I've been gone a long time . . ."

"It's okay, Don," Linda said, rubbing his arms.

"It's not okay!"

"It's okay because we got you back," Linda said, lovingly but with a hint of stern appeal. "The important thing is that you're here with your boys now, Don, and they all turned out great. They're wonderful."

"Oh, Don, they're the best kids," Teresa chimed in.

"Yeah, but I missed them all growing up," Donny said. He was not accepting that it had really been ten years. Linda accentuated the positive. "They have a lot of years left and you do, too. From now on you aren't going to miss anything, okay?"

"Donny?! Where's Donny?" he blurted, as it dawned on him that his oldest boy was absent.

"Are you sitting down?" Simon cracked.

Linda finished: "He's in India."

Donny's eyebrows raised to this latest splash of peculiarity, and he responded without missing a beat.

"Holy shit."

DON HERBERT JR. and his traveling companion, Wade, had planned to continue westward across India toward New Delhi, and eventually on to Bombay. They essentially had been following the Ganges River by train, starting on the east coast in Calcutta. In the weeks prior, they had hiked in the foothills of the Himalayas, leaving from Darjeeling, a few hundred miles south of Nepal. One morning before sunrise, Don hiked up to a bluff where he had a clear view of Mount Everest. No one had understood why a guy like him—who hated crowds and cities—would ever want to go to India. He could never explain his logic, that when you got outside the cities you found vistas like the one on that morning, just mountains and endless sky, for as far as the eyes could see. It seemed like heaven on earth.

"Hey, I'm going to check my e-mail," Wade said.

By chance they had stumbled down an alleyway that led to an Internet café. It might be weeks before they found another one. Since Wade was going in anyway, Don thought he might as well, too.

As NIGHT FELL on Father Baker Manor, the visitors continued to pour in. Jean and Tom Finn came with their newest addition, eight-week-old Billy, who cried in Donny's arms. A smile crossed Donny's face.

"It's nice to hear the sound of a baby's cry, isn't it, Don?" Linda asked.

Donny had a bulletin board in his room filled with Christmas card photos of all the cousins and nieces and nephews he'd never met, but who all knew him. Now they'd get a chance to really get to know him, Linda thought.

He continued to struggle with the reality that he'd been gone for so long. He also appeared to have trouble retaining information, as if the well of short-term memory had dried up. The news of his lengthy retreat from his family's lives kept splashing over him, triggering tears and tortured expressions. At one point he turned to Linda and gasped: "How have you survived without me?"

"I tell you, Donny, it wasn't always easy," Linda explained. "But I had *so* much support from family and friends, you wouldn't believe it. Everybody helped us, Don. Everybody. We had a big benefit for you at the Aud. Simon was there, the guys from the fire department—no one forgot about you, *no one*. You have friends and people who care about you that you never even knew you had."

"Wow," was all Donny could reply.

It was the same response when he was told that Linda's sister Debbie had married an Englishman and had a daughter in kindergarten; that Simon's oldest boy went to the University of Virginia; that Tommy had a girlfriend.

"You want to meet her?" Tommy asked.

Caitlin stepped forward.

"Hi, Mr. Herbert. I'm Caitlin Fitzpatrick," she said, positioning herself in front of his wheelchair. "We've been going out since high school. I've been taking good care of him."

Voices came at Donny from all directions, each nugget of information exploding in his head. As rational as he could sound, his logic was befuddled. For example, it never once occurred to him to ask why he had been unconscious, nor to inquire what had happened, and no one told him. Linda simply said he'd hit his head and lost his memory.

Donny responded to questions and updates the best he could, at times displaying humor and concern. When informed that Linda still received a paycheck from the fire department, Donny cracked, "I'll have to thank somebody for that." But through it all he kept asking for Linda and the kids. He continued to reach out for them, at one point crying, "Where is my wife? I love her . . ."

"I'm right here, Don," Linda replied.

He hugged her with those arms, not as powerful as they once were but still strong, and he refused to let her go.

"Are you comfortable in the chair, or would you like to move to the recliner?" Linda asked.

"I don't care where I sit," Donny said. "As long as I have you."

GOSSIP SPREAD IN South Buffalo pretty quickly, but word that Donny Herbert had woken up traveled at warp speed—across the fire department station houses to corner taverns, to households, church parking lots, cell phone to cell phone, each caller having to swear to the rumor's authenticity.

Donny's room at Father Baker Manor continued to swell up with loved ones and friends, as firemen like Gary O'Neill and Mike Lombardo arrived. Simon had left Dr. Ahmed several messages; as it turned out he and his family were away visiting one of his brothers in Toronto. Linda couldn't believe the nursing home wasn't able to get

Dr. Reilly to come out to examine Donny. But the doctor didn't work weekends, and, having had no prior contact with Donny, simply didn't grasp the enormity of the situation.

Donny kept a tight grip on Linda, who moderated his interactions skillfully and sensitively. But inside she was worried about what might come next. She knew there was no guarantee this would last. But she allowed herself to think—maybe.

"This is a miracle," she said to Donny as the night grew quiet and the room began to empty. "Do you know that? For you to come back to us after all this time . . . how many people get to say they experienced a miracle?"

Donny was calm now. The boys surrounded him.

"Patrick?"

"I'm here, Dad."

"Tommy . . . ?"

"Right behind you."

"I'm right here, too," Nick chimed in.

The boys' arms and Donny's intertwined in their clasp. Donny stared out ahead, basking in their love. Linda summed up what she thought he must have been thinking.

"Aren't we blessed?"

As THE NIGHT wore on, Donny did his best to catch up with all of his sons. He was still talking and making sense, and he refused to go to sleep. He wanted to keep on talking. But at around eleven P.M., when Linda suggested that she and the boys should go home and try to let him get some sleep, Donny began to panic. They stayed a little longer. Patrick told him tales of bow hunting—he'd bagged a few bucks with his bow and arrow. Donny was impressed; he'd gotten a few bucks with his shotgun, but never with the bow, and not for lack of trying.

It was decided that Patrick would spend the night with him, in the comfy blue recliner. Linda promised to return in the morning.

"We have every day to look forward to now," she said. "From now on, you'll never miss anything else. You'll never be alone, okay?"

Linda knew her night was not over; she'd be unable to sleep. She had to try to contact Don junior, and her best chance was by e-mail.

Hopefully, he would get it soon and could return home quickly, while his dad was still speaking, but she couldn't be sure.

DON LOGGED ON to the computer in the Varanasi Internet café and called up his Yahoo account. It took a few minutes. Right away, he noticed a few pieces of spam and two e-mails from his mom.

Don read the first one. The subject line read: "Great news." As he read the words his mother had written to him, the scruffy adventurer remained calm and thought one of two things had taken place thousands of miles away back in Buffalo: His father really had woken up from his nightmarish stupor—or his mother had completely lost her mind. Either way, he had to get home.

NO MATTER HOW HARD he tried, Patrick Herbert couldn't get his dad to go to sleep. Donny wanted to keep talking, and then he would grow panicky and ask for Linda. It was a long night of Patrick doing his best to keep him relaxed, often having to repeat to him what was going on.

Around five-thirty A.M., Donny was still calling out for Linda. Patrick got up from the recliner and stood over his father's bed. Donny seemed scared.

"Lin, where are you?" he asked. "Lin?!"

Patrick did his best to calm him down.

"Dad, come on, you have to get some sleep."

"Patrick?"

Though Patrick had already told his father the story earlier, he knew he could get away with telling it again. Outside, the first light of day was forcing its way across the tree line, Chestnut Ridge in the distance.

"Did I tell you about the time I got my first buck?"

"A buck? Wow."

"Got it with the bow."

Donny was calm again, fighting to stay awake but lying down, still, beginning to breathe deeply. Patrick whispered to him the story of getting his first buck, sparing no details. It was something he was particularly proud of, something he'd always wanted to share with his father. Patrick always figured he would never get the chance. One more telling of the story was fine by him, exhausted as he was after such a long day and night.

"It was three years ago. I was out on Uncle Pete Terzian's land—"

"Uncle Pete . . ."

"The sun had just come up, and I was sitting in a tree stand. It was quiet. You would have loved it."

Donny's eyes started to flutter.

"I heard a crackling and a doe ran by. All of a sudden there it was, a buck, I'd say fifteen feet away. . . ."

Donny turned his head now, struggling to listen.

"I knew I didn't have much time, so I just took aim and . . . I dropped it, Dad.

"I dropped it. You should have seen it."

Patrick finished the story as the dawn broke outside. And Donny Herbert, awake and talking for nearly sixteen hours after so many years of silence, peacefully drifted off to sleep.

Epilogue

ONNY SLEPT FOR the better part of the next day and a half, lingering in an undisturbed slumber worthy of an Egyptian pharaoh. Linda sat by his bedside. Outside the hallways and rooms of Father Baker Manor, the story of his dramatic reawakening spread like wildfire, beyond the city of Buffalo, over radio, to local papers and the Associated Press, the major news websites, and then on to television. In less than forty-eight hours, the entire world knew of the unbelievable event in Buffalo, New York.

On Monday, May 2, Donny finally stirred. He talked a bit more, but not nearly as much as he had during his amazing outburst on Saturday. But he was talking and he was following commands, albeit sluggishly.

Dr. Eileen Reilly, who served as a resident physician on the Opal wing of Father Baker Manor, examined Donny and immediately raised the idea of beginning structured speech therapy. Linda was full-throttle emboldened for anything now, and began to think about returning Donny to the Lake Erie Institute of Rehabilitation, perhaps as soon as that very week.

More visitors came, even as Donny slept. Father Joe Bayne came by and tearfully gave Linda a hug. He hadn't been around much lately, torn by his own grief and competing allegiances. Linda, as always taking the high road, let him know she more than understood. Donny slept. *Good Morning America* called, as did CNN, but Donny just slept. He and his miracle were cocooned. Apart from a brief statement Uncle Simon read to the media at the nursing home, the world would have to wait for more details. This was the family's time.

By Monday afternoon, Donny was withdrawn, exhausted by too much activity. Dr. Ahmed, who had heard the news on the radio earlier that morning while driving in his car, found himself tangled in procedural red tape just to obtain permission to examine Donny at the nursing home. Meanwhile, people were still coming by; some of them Linda politely turned away. Late in the day, Donny received a visit from the other Father Joe, the Buffalo police chaplain, Father Joe Moreno, the jolly round priest with the bushy hair whom the kids had nicknamed Father Cannoli.

"Can I just say hello?" he asked Linda. "I'll only be a minute."

"Of course," Linda said.

She was out in the hall talking on the phone to Simon's wife, Kathy, who was manning the Durant Street fort—fielding hundreds of calls from newspaper reporters and television producers around the world, dutifully writing down their names and numbers in a blue binder while explaining it was a time of privacy for the family. Some in the media thrust the feel-good story upon a deliberate backdrop: the highly politicized, heart-wrenching demise of brain-damaged Terri Schiavo, which had occurred just a month or so before. Others interpreted Donny Herbert's reawakening as a sign of the preciousness of life, as nothing short of a miracle.

Linda was trying to contact Dr. Ahmed and sort out the next step of rehab for Donny. She was also worried about Don junior. She knew the story was breaking on the news channels, and she needed to get in touch with him. Maybe the U.S. consulate could help.

Father Joe Moreno bounded out of Donny's room in a sweaty, trembling bluster, nearly knocking Linda out of his way.

"What's the matter?" Linda asked, in the midst of a cell phone conversation. She only half understood his response.

"I-I-I have to go see Monsignor Wurtz," Father Moreno said nervously. "Don just told me that *he saw Father Baker.*"

LINDA AND SIMON took turns guarding the doors as reporters and cameramen swarmed the facility. Producers from *Dateline, 60 Minutes,* the *Today Show, Nightline,* the BBC all reached out for interviews. Linda declined each one; she was not ready. A *National Enquirer* correspondent cased out their Durant Street home. Dozens of reporters hung outside the nursing home trying to cajole updates from staffers, who to a person refused to oblige. Finally, on Wednesday, May 4, at the suggestion of Simon, who'd consulted an old friend who did Beltway public relations, Linda read a brief statement during a news conference at the Erie County Medical Center. Tommy stood behind her, while Dr. Jamil Ahmed and Dr. Eileen Reilly were on hand to answer reporters' questions.

Shutters and flashbulbs popping in front of her, Linda began: "As you can imagine, for us to speak to and be recognized by my husband, their father, after nine and a half years, was completely overwhelming. We are still trying to cope with this incredible experience."

Dr. Ahmed, taken aback by his sudden celebrity but graceful in the spotlight, was asked about his drug cocktail, but he declined to be specific. "I can say that one of them is commonly used to treat Parkinson's and another to treat attention deficit hyperactivity disorder," he explained. When prodded for more specifics—could he say definitively that it was the cocktail that brought Donny back to life?—the doctor hedged.

"I would say this is a result of the combination of the drugs and God's help."

Later, Dr. Reilly, who'd only been working with Donny a short time, took a crack at one of the most difficult questions of all.

"Was it a miracle?" Gene Warner, a *Buffalo News* reporter, asked, pulling her aside after the press conference had wrapped up.

All week, faithful supporters of Father Baker and Buffalo-area Catholics were abuzz with speculation over the connection between the nursing home called Father Baker Manor and Donny Herbert's one-in-a-million triumph over what seemed a hopeless condition. For her part, Linda truly believed it *was* a miracle, though she had prayed to every saint and holy figure on record. But beyond her prepared statement, she stayed quiet.

Dr. Reilly responded to the reporter's question by saying simply: "I can't explain it any other way."

LATER THAT NIGHT, in the early morning hours of Thursday, May 5, Don Herbert Jr. scared the hell out of his little brother Nick as he came up the stairs, stinking to high heaven. He hadn't told anyone he was coming home; well, not exactly true. He'd e-mailed his aunt Debbie to alert her.

But he hadn't told his mom, reasoning that if he e-mailed her he was coming home, she might feel guilty over ruining his trip, as farfetched as that logic might seem.

But he also wanted to surprise her. Another factor was that he didn't want to overpromise, such was the hassle of getting to New Delhi, then on a flight from London to JFK. Smelling like a dead animal, his clothes and hair a tribute to filth, Don junior had finally made it home.

Linda heard Nicky's shout and got up from her bed. As soon as she saw Don junior, she hugged him and they both cried.

"I'm sorry I wasn't here," he said.

"Don't be," Linda told him. "You'll get your chance to talk to Dad."

LATER THAT WEEK, Donny Herbert sat in his wheelchair in the courtyard outside his room at Father Baker Manor. He was no longer speaking much, but remarkably, he was able to throw a football. And not just pathetic tosses, but well-aimed spirals, firing around from Nick to Patrick, everyone laughing, Linda amazed at his dexterity. He was fading, though, she could see it.

Right then, Dr. Ahmed came by for a surprise visit. "Hey, Donny," Linda said. "Meet Dr. Ahmed. He's the man who helped you."

Without uttering a word, Donny reached out and clutched the doctor by his shoulder, pulling him close, as if lifelong friends. As if, somehow, Donny *knew*.

Monsignor Wurtz made it known in interviews with local media that as head of Our Lady of Victory and chief advocate for the cause of Father Baker's canonization, he hoped to speak with Linda and the family about the recent events at the nursing home. But by Vatican stipulation, he couldn't call her; Linda had to reach out to him. Linda, busy with everything going on, heard that she was being summoned, but in truth, didn't see the point. What could she tell him anyway? She knew God was at work. But who was she to say if it was or wasn't a Father Baker miracle? Miracles happened every day in all shapes and sizes, she reasoned. She couldn't go out on this limb, in spite of what she privately believed.

Around Buffalo, however, an entire community, normally battered by media insults and sporting indignities, was feeling upbeat that a miracle—or at least something as close to one as anything else in recent memory—had occurred right in their own backyard.

Father Joe Moreno had phoned Monsignor Wurtz not long after running out of the nursing home that day. Wurtz, needless to say, had been skeptical. Stage two on Father Baker's road to sainthood—beatification—was one miracle away, yes, but this was high-stakes Catholicism. There could be no doubt.

"Are you sure that's what he said?"

"Yes, I'm sure."

To settle his nerves that day, Father Joe, who rarely

drank, had left Father Baker Manor and gone not to the
basilica or the OLV administrative headquarters, but to a
corner tavern near his East Side parish, where he summar-
ily downed three manhattans. He'd replayed the scene in
his mind, back in that room.

"How are you feeling, Donny?" Father Joe had asked.

At that moment, Donny seemed totally overcome,
engulfed in an indefinable yet palpable state of spiritual
awe, a state of grace perhaps, something Father Joe had
never witnessed in all of his priestly life, which as police
chaplain had involved administering last rites to scores of
accident victims on death's doorstep.

And Donny had said to him, as plain as day, "I saw
Father Baker."

Father Joe's heart began to thump, loud, rapid; he
thought he was having a panic attack. "Wh-what, Donny?
Are you sure?"

"Father Baker was in my room."

DOCTORS FROM AROUND the country contacted Linda
expressing interest in her husband's story and offering up
their services.

She chose the world-famous Rehabilitation Institute of
Chicago. However, right before Donny set off for Chicago,
he experienced an unfortunate setback, hitting his head
after falling in the nursing home. He was rushed to ECMC
with a gash that required stitches.

It is believed that he had another burst of cognition in the middle of the night and that he must have tried to get up from his bed when the mishap occurred. Later, the injury would be found to be more severe than initially thought. Follow-up CT scans revealed bleeding on the brain, exacerbated by the air pressure on the flight from Buffalo to Chicago. Progress, already slowing, declined further.

Donny spoke far less frequently; in truth, his subsequent communications were nothing like that incredible first day, but he was still visibly fighting. In Chicago, Linda had stayed in his room, sleeping on a loveseat. She saw just how hard Donny worked, just how tired he really was. She went through entire days with him, unbearably grueling therapy, hours and hours of it, feedings, changings, speech rehab, examinations. For Donny, every single thing seemed a herculean labor. But he didn't give up.

Some generous members of the Chicago Fire Department heard about Donny's story and arranged for Linda to stay at a Sheraton Hotel two blocks from the rehab center. The department's Gold Badge Society, an organization formed as a support group for the widows and families of fallen firemen, also took Linda under their wing, making sure her every need was met. GBS members Father Tom Mulcrone and Eileen Coglianese quickly became extended family. Eventually, Linda went back to staying with Donny in his room. On Father's Day, Nick, Tommy, and Patrick again and joined Linda by Donny's side.

By the end of the summer of 2005, Donny had slipped away again. He was transferred to St. Camillus Health and Rehabilitation Center in Syracuse for further therapy; at least it was closer to Buffalo. But when Donny regressed further, back to the point where he was before his reawakening, Linda found the closest nursing home she could, Ridgeview Manor, on the corner of Dorrance and McKinley in South Buffalo, a five-minute drive from her home. Not much longer after that, sadly, Linda's father, as she once feared, became a resident there, too.

Linda found it hard to explain to people that Donny wasn't doing so well. Once again it was hard on the boys, but thanks to Linda they kept their hopes in check, even if many others assumed that it was only a matter of time before Donny would be back mowing the lawn or fixing their roofs.

AND THEN, sudden and swift, on a Saturday evening in late February 2006, Donny Herbert came down with pneumonia and spiked a fever. He was rushed to Mercy Hospital and drenched in ice. Right away Linda had a bad feeling. His breathing was shallow, and his doctors looked worried.

She called the boys one at a time, urging them to come visit their father. In spite of her growing concern that this could be the end, Linda did not tip her hand. He'd pull through, she thought. But when Donny's temperature reached 105 degrees, despite the ice-down and a flurry of antibiotics, Linda knew. She just knew.

The following Monday afternoon, she called Tommy, who was now a police officer in Atlanta.

"You'd better come home," Linda said. "I don't know if your dad is going to make it this time."

Firemen heard the grave word, that their comrade was failing, and by the dozen they showed up at Mercy to see him, some coming directly from an East Side fire. Linda smelled the heavy smoke scent and thought back to that morning at ECMC in 1995, when all those firemen in their turnout coats lined the hallways. Now it was happening all over again. In a weird way, it was as if the past ten years had been one long day.

At around ten P.M. the nurses suggested that Linda and the boys say their good-byes. Father Adolph, from St. Agatha's, came to give Donny last rites. But he hung on, fighting until just after twelve-thirty A.M., when Tommy finally made it there, having caught, with five minutes to spare, the last flight from Atlanta to Buffalo.

With Linda and the last of his four boys by his side, Donny Herbert finally gave up. He passed away on Tuesday, February 21, just before two A.M. He was forty-four years old.

THE FUNERAL WAS HELD on Saturday, February 25, 2006. In one of the biggest Buffalo processions in recent memory, Donny Herbert was memorialized at a Mass at the Our Lady of Victory Basilica. Traffic was tied up for miles. More than seven hundred firemen from all over the country came to pay their respects. Practically the entire BFD provided an honor guard, standing for hours in the freezing morning, unflinching, proud to be a part of the salute. Linda and the boys entered the magnificent basilica, which was filled from front to back, with firemen pouring onto Ridge Road. She huddled together with her sons, who practically held her upright by the back of her black wool coat.

During the funeral Mass, Mike Lombardo, who had just been named the Buffalo fire commissioner, recalled Donny's struggle to hang on until of all his boys could be there to say their good-byes. "He was," Lombardo said, "a fighter till the end."

Before the funeral was over, Linda was presented with an American flag.

NO ONE WHO witnessed it will ever forget the day Donny Herbert woke up. Whether it was Dr. Ahmed's drug cocktail, the intercession of Father Baker, an act of God himself, or a combination of all three, Linda tends to credit Donny. It was Donny who overcame a brain that did not work, Donny who had the strength and the love to will himself back into his family's lives, if only momentarily.

Monsignor Robert Wurtz never did follow up on the curious claim made by Father Joe Moreno, explaining to the subordinate clergyman that in actuality it was more likely that Dr. Ahmed's "miracle drug cocktail" and not the intercession of Father Baker had brought Donny back from his unresponsive stupor. The Vatican had strict rules, he explained, and any shred of associated medical explanation automatically rendered such a claim useless in the eyes of the Vatican, insofar as proving a miracle. Chagrined, Father Joe told a few close confidants of his encounter, but for the most part let it rest.

In early December 2006, Monsignor Wurtz died after a battle with cancer. Prayers to Father Baker helped him through his long fight, or at least that's what he and many believed. He died not knowing whether Father Baker would be advanced to the next step on the road to sainthood, beatification. As of this writing, the Vatican has not yet made any decision.

On a bitterly cold Sunday in January 2007, nearly a year after Donny's death, Linda Herbert attended the eleven o'clock Mass at St. Agatha's Church. It was no basilica, but it was comforting. She found herself listening intently to one of the readings, 1 Corinthians 12:31–13:13, one she had heard many times before, primarily at weddings. In fact, it had been a reading at her own wedding twenty-five years earlier.

"In this life we have three lasting qualities—faith, hope, and love. But the greatest of these is love."

It had, in all honesty, not meant very much to her back then. Of course she and Donny loved each other. But now as the priest, Father Adolph, expounded upon the theme of faith, hope, and love in his sermon, Linda was moved, not by closure—she would never get over losing Donny—but by a feeling that was closer to a moment of clarity.

After everything Linda had been through, those words of Saint Paul in his letter to the Corinthians truly resonated. She did have faith; she did have hope. And Donny's love did come through in the end—for her and her boys.

ACKNOWLEDGMENTS

This book could not have been written without the full cooperation of Linda Herbert. Her willingness to recall and speak openly about painful memories and events was crucial to this chronicling. A special thanks, also, to the Herbert boys—Donny, Tommy, Patrick, and Nicholas—all of whom came through for me time and again.

My gratitude is owed to the Buffalo Fire Department, beginning with Commissioner Mike Lombardo and his assistant, Joyce Whitman, as well as several current and former members of Rescue 1, specifically John Breier, Pat Coghlan, Jerry Nostrant, and Bill Sanford. Thanks also to Gary O'Neill, Greg Pratchett, Larry Robertson, Dave Rowley, and Jim Seemueller.

For medical issues, I benefited greatly from the invaluable assistance and unwavering patience of two practitioners—Dr. Jamil Ahmed and Dr. Nicholas Schiff. Additionally, I'd like to thank the staff of Father Baker Manor, especially Michael McRae, Patricia Fernandes, and Lynn Hornberger.

The following individuals were also very helpful: Father Joe Bayne, Debbie Corbett, Mary Blake, Patrick Blake, Teresa Blake, Bob Bruenn, Monsignor Al Clody, Margaret Coghlan, Joe Corey, Beth Donovan, Mike Faliero, Caitlin Fitzpatrick, Joe Foley, Rick Insalaco, Cornelius Keane, Richard Keane, Skip Kessler, Jim and Ellen Kolb, Randall Lane, Carrie Lynch, Simon and Kathy Manka, Father Joe Moreno, Terri Schuta, Don Stoeckel, Dr. Matt O'Hearn, Father Joe Penkaul, Luanne Schipani, and Monsignor Robert Wurtz, may he rest in peace.

I'd like to thank my mother, Patricia Stewart, for relenting on her threats in the mid-1970s to send me away to Father Baker's orphanage. Her toughness became mine, which helped in the stressful times that can accompany writing a book.

And finally, a very, very special thanks to my aide de camp/researcher extraordinaire and love, Meryl Paula Kaye.